Interval Training for Fitness

Joseph T. Nitti and Kimberlie Nitti

London: A & C Black,
2002

0713663820

Published in 2002 by
A & C Black Publishers Ltd
37 Soho Square, London W1D 3QZ
www.acblack.com

First published in 2001 by
Hunter House Inc., Publishers
PO Box 2914
Alameda CA 94501-0914

ISBN 0 7136 6382 0

A CIP catalogue record for this book is available from the British Library.

Note: Whilst every effort has been made to ensure that the content of this book is as technically accurate and as sound as possible, neither the authors nor the publishers can accept responsibility for any injury or loss sustained as a result of the use of this material.

A&C Black uses paper produced with elemental chlorine-free pulp, harvested from managed sustainable forests.

Cover images © ImageState

Typeset in 11/12pt Minion Display

Printed and bound in Great Britain by Biddles Ltd, Guildford and Kings Lynn

Contents

Acknowledgements

We wish to thank the many friends and family members who generously played a part in making this book possible. Most of all, we are grateful to all our models, whom we shamelessly strong-armed into service: Mark Luevano, Annetta Luevano, Dr Gary Nitti, Wendi Nitti, and Vic Simonian. Thanks also to Joe Douglas of the Santa Monica Track Club, Carl Lewis, Jenny Spangler, Anne Marie Fox, Mattias Persson, Michael Gunn, Melanie Winstead, and Chuch Crossland of 24-Hour Fitness/Santa Monica.

Important Note

The material in this book is intended to provide a review of information regarding fitness training. Every effort has been made to provide accurate and dependable information, and the contents of this book have been compiled through professional research and in consultation with medical professionals. However, always consult your doctor before undertaking a new exercise regime or doing any of the exercises – or following the suggestions – contained in this book.

The authors, publisher, editors and professionals quoted in the book cannot be held responsible for any error, omission or dated material in the book. The author and publisher are not liable for any damage or injury or other adverse outcome of applying the information in this book in an exercise programme carried out independently or under the care of a licensed trainer or practitioner. If you have questions concerning the application of the information described in this book, consult a qualified and trained professional.

Foreword

Carl Lewis

As a world-class athlete and Olympic champion, I've found that people around the world are curious to peek inside the head of an elite athlete and find an answer to one particular question: what's the secret?

The truth is, there isn't one.

I didn't win those medals because I trained at altitude, or had to run back and forth to school as a child, or took any performance-enhancing drugs or supplements. There are only three things that make a great athlete: good genes, a strong work ethic, and an intelligent, well-crafted training programme.

It's been said, 'To become an Olympic athlete, choose your parents well.' There may come a day when genetic engineering is perfected, but for now we all have to work with what we're born with. What you *can* control is how hard you are willing to work for your physical goals.

It isn't easy, pushing your body to higher heights, faster times, greater distances. There have been many, many days when I felt too tired or too sore to work out or just plain didn't feel like doing it. But I did it anyway. That's what you do if you want to win gold at the Games or attain a personal best in a sport or just make your body fitter and stronger than ever before. Working hard and, even more importantly, working *smart* – this is truly the stuff of champions.

Not everyone can be an elite athlete. But knowing how to train like one, that's a whole different story. *Interval Training for Fitness* is the next best thing to having your very own coach. The techniques found in this book aren't new or revolutionary, as interval training has been used for decades by the world's greatest athletes. What is special about this book is that it presents interval training as a complete programme for athletes of *all* abilities. *Interval Training for Fitness* can teach you how to train like a world-class athlete – the rest is up to you. If you can dream great dreams and have the dedication, courage, and determination to make them come true, you can be one of the few to reach your full physical potential. Who knows how far you'll go? Set your goals high – then go out and attain them. That's what being an athlete is all about.

Carl Lewis has won more Olympic gold medals than any American in history. He has been ranked number one in the world in the 100 metres, 200 metres, and long jump multiple times. He is considered by many to be one of the greatest athletes of all time.

Preface

It's not the years, it's the mileage.

– Indiana Jones

Despite the overwhelming hype and promise of the fitness boom, most people never meet their fitness and weight loss goals. The complaints are all too common: 'I run 15 miles a week but I haven't lost any more weight.' Or, 'How can I still be out of shape when I work out on the stair climber 30 minutes every day?'

Why is this?

It's because most people do no more than mildly exert themselves at the same comfortable, steady pace each time they work out. It may work for a while, but as millions of frustrated exercisers have discovered, it doesn't work for long. The unfortunate thing is that most people have never been taught how to improve.

What is clearly needed is an exercise routine that:

- is scientifically and clinically proven to build muscle, burn fat, and improve the body's cardiovascular system

- can be adapted for use with different aerobic activities, such as running, walking, cycling, or swimming or for workouts using fixed exercise machines (such as stair climbers, stationary bicycles, treadmills, cross-country ski machines, or elliptical trainers)

- doesn't require any special or expensive equipment

- can be done alone or with others

- is designed so you can progress at your own pace

- can be used by anyone in reasonable health with a basic foundation of fitness

- offers a variety of workouts to keep things interesting

- provides a clear measure of physical improvement

- gives maximum results in minimal time

These very elements form the basis of the I.T. programme, a practical, easy-to-understand, scientifically and clinically proven fitness plan based on the training methods used by the fittest, leanest people on earth: elite athletes.

I.T. stands for 'interval training', a technique originally developed in the 1930s. Until then, athletic training for endurance events was a bit haphazard, and many athletes who found their way to the top of the awards podium were victorious simply because they had the good fortune to have superior genetics. You either had it from birth or you didn't – the ability to go faster wasn't considered attainable by any other means.

Fortunately, two German track coaches dared to think differently. As exercise physiologists, they had a theory that if a runner practised doing brief segments of his regular workouts at a faster 'race pace', he could later string together all those fast segments in actual competition to achieve a better overall time.

It worked. Varying the degree of effort used within a single workout (fast 'repetitions' followed by slower recovery 'intervals') produced spectacular results. World records began to improve dramatically and athletes all over the world scrambled to adopt the revolutionary interval training method for themselves. One such individual was British medical student Roger Bannister. In 1954, after using the principles of I.T. in his daily one hour training regime, he went on to be the first in the world to run a mile in under 4 minutes. This set an exciting new benchmark for athletic achievement – and human potential.

Today, every top endurance runner, cyclist and swimmer aiming for peak performance uses some form of interval training. That's a good enough recommendation for us. But what if you're not an elite athlete? No problem. The same physiologic principles apply to almost everyone, from weekend enthusiasts to national-class marathon runners. It's not necessary to be in stellar shape to benefit from interval training. Just the opposite, in fact: the I.T. programme is designed to help you attain superior fitness.

Until now, there's never been a single, authoritative source that presented the basic training principles of elite athletes in a way that could be adapted by others interested in better health and fitness. But after Joseph qualified for the '92 Olympic Trials, so many people began to ask for advice about their own training that we started writing down our notes, and the I.T. programme slowly began to take shape. Those who were motivated enough to follow the programme described in this book went on to achieve – and sometimes even surpass – their health and fitness goals. We were motivated to publish the I.T. programme because it worked for them, and we're confident it can work for you, too.

Joseph and Kimberlie Nitti

I.T. basics: the science behind the fitness

Over the years, various fitness 'gurus' have had a major influence on the British public, offering a fitness programme designed to improve health, build muscle, and burn calories. Each one of these exercise entrepreneurs became a household name to thousands of faithful fans. But, oddly enough, the person who probably had the most influence on fitness might very well be someone you've never even heard of.

Dr Kenneth Cooper launched one of the biggest fitness revolutions in history with his book *Aerobics*, published in the late 1960s. Cooper's book popularised the notion that moderate aerobic exercise (strictly defined as exercise done 'with oxygen') performed three to four times a week for 20 minutes was all it took to improve health and fitness. Aerobics became hugely popular and inspired the jogging craze of the 1970s and the 'power walking' fad that followed. People were understandably enthused about an exercise plan that required little more than lacing up a pair of trainers, wasn't too physically taxing, didn't take all day and even packed a bit of an endorphin kick. It sounded like the discovery of the Holy Grail of physical fitness, and, to some degree, it was. Aerobic devotees enjoy fairly decent returns for their rather minimal efforts, becoming fitter, managing their weight better and enjoying healthier lives.

In fact, aerobics has become such a part of the cultural lexicon that today the very word calls to mind images of lycra-clad bodies sweating to the beat of loud music in packed exercise studios. But the aerobics movement also includes the many dedicated fitness buffs who run, walk, cycle, swim and use fixed exercise machines. This massive group of well-intentioned, health-oriented individuals probably includes you, the reader of this book.

So the question is, with all this exercising going on why aren't there more people out there in better shape?

Two words: Plateau effect.

The plateau effect

The 'plateau effect' is a rather disheartening levelling off of fitness as measured by such things as exercise tolerance, weight control, and athletic performance. Anyone who works out consistently has probably experienced this dreaded plateau to some degree. You're exercising as much as ever, but instead of improving, you're unable to budge those last few kilos or advance to a tougher level of step class or swim a mile any faster than you could swim it months ago.

Why is this?

It's because your exercise programme is too limited.

The bottom line is that purely aerobic exercise can only take the body so far, even if you had a whole day, every day, to devote to working out. Relying solely on moderately paced, moderately difficult exercise, as most people do, will never, ever give you anything more substantial than (yawn) moderate results. You'll definitely be in better shape than a beer-swilling, channel-surfing couch potato, of course, but you won't ever be considered very fit. Unfortunately, most people have never been taught to exercise any other way.

Does aerobic exercise work? Of course. But interval training works better.

Interval training (I.T.) makes the most of the limited amount of time most of us have available for exercise. Instead of squandering this time on comfort zone exercise, the I.T. programme devotes a couple sessions a week to more challenging workouts. These workouts use brief bursts of higher-intensity activity to generate powerful physiologic processes, which result in decreased body fat and increased fitness and strength. I.T. helps you get the most out of the time you have and ultimately rewards you with better results.

I.T. v aerobic exercise

There is no question that interval training is superior to purely aerobic exercise. This has been proven both in the stadium and in the laboratory. Basically, I.T. delivers remarkable results by using the body's natural ability to adapt to physical stress. The I.T. programme is based primarily on several scientifically proven mechanisms.

I.T. increases human growth hormone

One way the body deals with the stress of higher intensity exercise is by secreting hormones, such as Human Growth Hormone (HGH). This naturally occurring anabolic (or 'building') hormone stimulates muscle growth by encouraging the creation of protein. HGH also makes fats more available as fuel for the body by increasing their presence in the bloodstream. Simply put, HGH builds muscle and burns fat, which is exactly what most people are looking to get out of their workout programme. Several experts have even touted HGH as the secret to slowing the ageing process and enjoying a longer, fuller life. It's not too surprising that some Olympic-calibre athletes have been banned for cheating with illegal injections of HGH.

Fortunately, you can steer clear of needles and get the same performance-enhancing benefits by doing interval training, which increases HGH. Blood levels of HGH have been shown to rise significantly during and immediately after interval training. This is substantially different from purely aerobic exercise, in which HGH levels remain the same both during and after a workout. No matter what level of fitness you're at or what type of exercise you do, I.T. boosts HGH production like no other legal substance. I.T. also releases other useful hormones such as corticotropin, cortisol and catecholamines, all of which help to mobilise fats as a source of energy.

The power 'A's: ATP, Aerobic and Anaerobic

The words 'cellular metabolism' may trigger haunting memories of high school biology class, with all those charts of Kreb's Cycles and other scary stuff that you promptly forgot after final exams. For anyone serious about athletics, however, a simple explanation of how the power 'A's generate energy within exercising muscles might be interesting.

For starters, you need to know that ATP stands for **adenosine triphosphate**, and an ATP molecule is the basic unit of cellular energy. Say you're walking down a street. In order to move, ATP needs to be broken down in the muscles to provide the required energy. But there are only a few seconds worth of ATP available in your cells, so more has to be made, pronto – otherwise you'll stop moving. The primary energy provider, **aerobic metabolism**, kicks in. Aerobic means 'with oxygen', and aerobic metabolism combines oxygen with carbohydrates, fats, and proteins to create ATP. Aerobic metabolism is pretty darn efficient, in that it can produce a whopping 38 ATP by combining a single molecule of glucose (a form of carbohydrate) with oxygen. Since there's an abundance of oxygen available when you're walking at an easy pace, you can keep creating enough ATP to plod along for quite some time.

Now say you start jogging. The faster pace requires more energy, which means there's less oxygen available for use. You start breathing harder, trying to get more oxygen into your lungs, and your heart rate speeds up to deliver that oxygen to working muscle cells. The oxygen then moves to the cell 'powerhouses' (mitochondria), to crank out enough ATP to meet the muscles' energy needs. This is considered an aerobic workout, exercise that is done at an intensity that can be adequately fuelled with oxygen.

Pick up the pace to a sprint. Now you are generating maximum ATP using oxygen (i.e. aerobically), but it just isn't enough to maintain the higher speed. Here's where the anaerobic system kicks in. **Anaerobic metabolism** converts carbohydrates and some fats into ATP without using any oxygen whatsoever and provides enough energy to keep you sprinting for a short time. But there's a cost. For one thing, the anaerobic system is extremely inefficient—it can only generate a measly two (two!) ATP from a molecule of glucose. It also produces lactic acid, a nasty substance that causes your legs to burn after a short burst of sprinting. Eventually, the acidity shuts down muscle cell activity, causing your muscles to fail and forcing you to slow down. This allows the lactic acid to disperse and recovery to occur as oxygen levels catch up again to meet the body's energy needs. For all its limitations, the anaerobic system is the primary way to create energy in larger muscle fibres during very high-intensity activity, such as interval training.

I.T. burns calories

I.T. gets you exercising at higher intensities for brief chunks of time. This extra effort takes more energy than the plodding pace of aerobic exercise because it taps larger, less efficient muscle fibres that aren't frequently used. And, using more energy means you're burning more calories.

Even better news: I.T. revs up your metabolism. After intense exercise, the body needs extra calories as it works to repair muscles, replenish energy stores and restore the body to its normal state again. Since this can take from several hours to a full day, you'll keep on burning calories long after the workout is over. That doesn't happen with purely aerobic exercise. Over the course of the I.T. programme, resting metabolism increases along with lean muscle mass, because muscle needs additional calories to fuel its everyday metabolic functions. All this calorie burning and muscle building ultimately results in a leaner, fitter body. You can't beat that.

I.T. taps larger muscle fibres

Interval training requires both small and large muscle fibres. Smaller muscle fibres are better at utilising oxygen and are employed mostly for aerobic exercise, while larger fibres generate more power and are used mainly for more strenuous anaerobic (meaning 'without oxygen') exercise. Since the larger fibres cannot use oxygen efficiently, they tend to fatigue quickly – which explains why you can only sprint so far, so fast, before you're exhausted and gasping desperately for air. Doing only moderate aerobic workouts all the time means that larger muscle fibres are more or less ignored, and they'll eventually shrink and weaken from lack of exercise. Use it or lose it, in other words. Interval training, on the other hand, uses both small and large muscle fibres. Making use of these larger fibres makes them more efficient and results in stronger muscles that are better able to handle heavy-duty exercise.

I.T. means greater fitness in less time

There's no question that aerobic exercise done regularly improves the body's cardiovascular system. But sooner or later there comes the dreaded fitness plateau, when improvement seems to grind to a halt. The I.T. programme is scientifically proven to break through this sort of barrier and provide you with greater fitness in less time. Studies of aerobically trained runners show that after a few months of interval training they are able to pump more blood and deliver more oxygen to their muscles, generating more energy than ever before. The I.T. programme also incorporates extra-long sessions of aerobic exercise – known as 'XL workouts' – which help the body generate energy in other ways. Here's how: during aerobic exercise, oxygen travels from the lungs via the blood to working muscles, where it's passed along from blood capillaries to muscle mitochondria (cell 'powerhouses' that use oxygen to convert food into energy). XL workouts help beef up capillary density and the number and size of mitochondria, so more oxygen can be used by the muscles, which results in more efficient energy production. Basically, having more energy to power a workout results in greater fitness for you, because you can exercise at higher intensities for longer periods of time.

With all this going for the I.T. programme, why wait? If you're anything like most people, you're looking for results, yesterday. Let's get started!

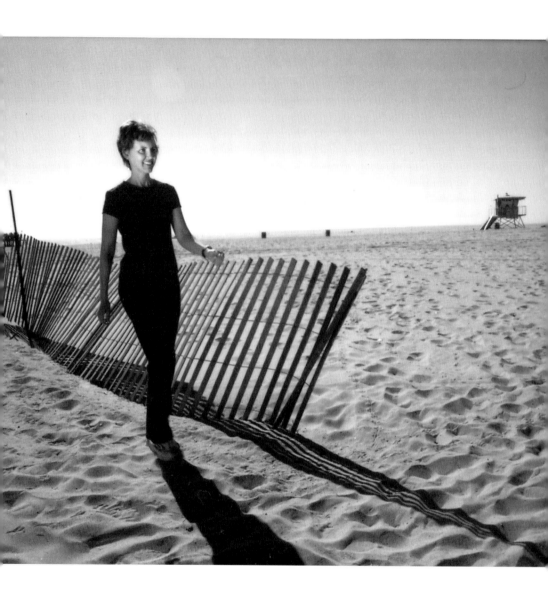

2 Before you start: building the foundation

The I.T. programme can benefit almost any healthy person, from beginning exercisers to world-class endurance athletes. In fact, most athletes you see participating in the Olympics or other major events use some form of interval training in their own workout programmes. That's not bad company to be in.

But even these paragons of fitness didn't start off doing I.T. from Day 1. They first had to develop a foundation of aerobic fitness that allowed them to physically and psychologically manage the higher intensity levels that interval training demands.

A consistent programme of aerobic exercise, even at a low level of effort, results in several encouraging changes:

• a more efficient heart and circulatory system

• improved oxygen delivery and utilisation by the muscles

• stronger muscles, tendons, ligaments and bones

• improved body composition (less fat and more muscle)

• better self-image and overall sense of well-being

Doing nothing but aerobic exercise may be enough for people who aren't out to become superfit. But for more motivated exercisers, aerobic training is mainly a springboard to the I.T. programme and its proven formula to control weight and attain maximum fitness.

Before starting the I.T. programme, you must be able to complete 30 minutes of continuous exercise at least three times a week for 4 consecutive weeks.

This continuous exercise can be any aerobic activity (such as walking, running, cycling, or using a stair climber) done at any intensity level, provided it lasts for 30 minutes. Already at this level of conditioning? You're probably ready to start doing I.T. If you don't have the recommended foundation yet, follow the aerobic base programme described later in this chapter. You'll be ready to step up to the I.T. programme in just 8 weeks. In either case, read the medical precautions section below before moving on to your first workout session.

Medical precautions

From blisters to stress fractures to heart attacks, there's always a possibility of some pain or injury with physical exertion. It may be necessary to get a green light from your doctor to ensure your body is up to the rigours of a new, strenuous exercise programme. The American College of Sports Medicine (ACSM) has two useful pre-exercise evaluations we've adapted here. They can help determine if you might be at risk for coronary artery disease or a disease of the cardiovascular and pulmonary systems.

Don't be overly concerned if you do need to see a doctor – a thorough medical history and physical exam may be all that's needed to get a thumbs-

Coronary artery disease risk factors

Family history: Heart attack, heart bypass surgery, or sudden death (due to cardiac arrest) before 55 years of age in father, brother or son, or before 65 years of age in mother, sister or daughter

Cigarette smoking: Current cigarette smoker or those who quit within the previous 6 months

High blood pressure: Systolic blood pressure (upper number) of greater than or equal to 140 mm Hg; or diastolic (lower number) blood pressure of greater than or equal to 90 mm Hg, confirmed by measurements on at least two separate occasions; or taking anti-hypertensive (high blood pressure) medication

High cholesterol: Total serum cholesterol of greater than 200 mg; or high-density lipoprotein cholesterol (HDL, or 'good' cholesterol) of less than 35 mg; or on lipid-lowering medication. If low-density lipoprotein cholesterol (LDL, or 'bad' cholesterol) measurement is available, use more than 130 mg as measure rather than total cholesterol of more than 200 mg

Impaired fasting glucose: Fasting blood glucose (test taken after 6 hours without food) of greater than or equal to 110 mg confirmed by measurements on at least two separate occasions

Obesity: Body Mass Index of greater than or equal to 30 kg/m squared (measured by taking your weight in kilograms and dividing it by your height in metres) or waist girth of more than approximately 40 inches

Sedentary lifestyle: Persons not participating in a regular exercise programme or meeting the minimal physical activity recommendations of 30 minutes or more of moderate physical activity on most days of the week.

*Reprinted with permission from JAMA and Lippincott Williams and Wilkins (*ACSM's Guidelines for Exercise Testing and Prescription, Sixth Edition*, American College of Sports Medicine, Lippincott Williams and Wilkins, Baltimore, Maryland, 2000)

Signs/symptoms of cardiovascular and pulmonary disease

- pain or discomfort in the chest, neck, jaw, arms, or other areas that may be angina ('heart pain' due to lack of oxygen)
- shortness of breath at rest or with mild exertion
- dizziness or fainting
- ankle edema (swelling)
- palpitations or tachycardia (rapid heart rate)
- orthopnea (shortness of breath when lying flat) or paroxysmal nocturnal dyspnea (awakening at night short of breath)
- intermittent claudication (pain in a limb with use, such as leg pain when walking)
- known heart murmur
- unusual fatigue or shortness of breath with usual activities

Consult your doctor before starting any new exercise programme if you:
- have any risk factors or symptoms listed above
- have diabetes or any known cardiovascular (heart), pulmonary (lung), hepatic (liver), renal (kidney), or thyroid disease
- are 70 years or older (your doctor may want to do a physical examination and perhaps some tests to rule out any disease that might be present but not causing symptoms)

Other age considerations:
If you are 45–70 years old and male, or 55–70 and female, without any of the listed risk factors or medical limitations, go ahead with low to moderate aerobic activity (defined by the ACSM as any comfortable level of intensity that can be sustained for up to 60 minutes, starting slowly and progressing gradually).

If you are 45 years or older and male, or 55 or older and female, or if you have two or more coronary disease risk factors, consult your doctor before doing any exercise vigorous enough to tire you after 20 minutes. Your age group is more at risk for underlying heart disease, so be sure to have a physical examination and an exercise stress test before starting the I.T. programme.

If you are younger than 45 years and male, or younger than 55 and female, with no more than one risk factor, move ahead with low to moderate aerobic exercise such as that found in the Aerobic Base Programme, outlined in this chapter. If you already have a solid aerobic foundation, you're ready to start the I.T. programme.

*Reprinted and adapted with permission from JAMA and Lippincott Williams and Wilkins (ACSM's Guidelines for Exercise Testing and Prescription, Sixth Edition, American College of Sports Medicine, Lippincott Williams and Wilkins, 2000) up to work out. Some simple blood tests or an electrocardiogram or a chest X ray may also be required, just to rule out the possibility of major organ disease (affecting such things as your heart, lungs, liver, kidneys, endocrine system or blood). Even if you feel perfectly healthy, you might need to do an exercise stress test if your doctor feels you may be at risk for myocardial ischemia (lack of oxygen to the heart) or heart failure (inability of the heart to manage exercise stress). A stress test simply involves walking or jogging on a treadmill while your heart is monitored for changes. The test may also include an echocardiogram to look for cardiac abnormalities such as decreased function and heart valve disease. It's a painless procedure done with a special probe (it looks like a small pressing iron) that's placed on your chest to generate an ultrasound image of the heart. Your doctor can interpret the results and help construct an exercise programme you can feel confident and comfortable doing.

Aerobic base programme

Don't worry if you suspect you aren't quite ready for interval training. If you don't have any medical limitations, the simple, 8 week aerobic base programme will get you on the road to better health and fitness. This programme, like the I.T. programme, is based on 'progressive overload', in which muscles are challenged with a gradually increasing level of effort over time. You start off easily and do a little more each week, factoring in some rest and recovery between steps, until you achieve your goal: 30 minutes of continuous aerobic activity, three to four times a week. Once you can do that, you're ready to move on to the full-fledged I.T. programme.

Here's how to get started.

First, choose a form of exercise. What interests you? What's most convenient? How available is equipment or a gym? If you like exercising outside, consider walking, jogging, swimming in a lake or outdoor pool or cycling on an open road or trail. If you prefer an indoor environment or a more social setting, try a well-equipped gym with treadmills, stair climbers, exercise bikes, cross-country ski machines or elliptical trainers. Some people use their local shopping centre as a warm, dry, safe place for a good brisk walk. If it works for you, why not? The idea is to choose an activity you can do consistently three to four days a week.

Start off doing just a single exercise, such as walking or cycling or stair climbing (later, when you start doing the I.T. programme, you may want to cross train by adding a few more activities). At this point, the level of intensity is not that important because your goal is merely a consistent 30 minute workout. (Once you can do that three to four times a week, and you don't have any medical limitations, you're ready to move on to the I.T. programme.) For now, just concentrate on completing the exercise at a pace that is comfortable – and enjoyable – for you.

There are a few things to keep in mind as you undertake this aerobic base programme.

Aerobic base programme

	Mon	Tue	Wed	Thur	Fri	Sat	Sun
Week 1	10 mins continuous activity	Rest	10 mins continuous activity	Rest	15 mins continuous activity	Rest	Rest
Week 2	15 mins continuous activity	Rest	15 mins continuous activity	Rest	20 mins continuous activity	Rest	Rest
Week 3	20 mins continuous activity	Rest	20 mins continuous activity	Rest	25 mins continuous activity	Rest	Rest
Week 4	25 mins continuous activity	Rest	25 mins continuous activity	Rest	30 mins continuous activity	Rest	Rest
Weeks 5 to 8	30 mins continuous activity	Rest	30 mins continuous activity	Rest	30 mins continuous activity	Rest day, or 15–30 mins continuous activity	Rest

If at any time you experience pain in your chest, jaw, upper back, or left arm, or a severe, sudden shortness of breath, stop immediately and call for medical assistance. These may be signs of myocardial ischemia (decreased oxygen supply to your heart).

If you are physically unable to complete a workout at any time during the first four weeks, decrease the effort level of the next workout or move back one week in the sequence.

Have fun! The time you spend doing this comfortably paced exercise can be used constructively to consider new ideas, come up with solutions for problems at home or at work, listen to favourite music, or even read magazines. Use it to clear your head or hang out with friends – taking a walk together instead of chatting over cups of coffee helps keep things interesting and gives an added boost of motivation, too.

Practical advice: shoes and clothing

When it comes to exercise, having the right shoes and athletic apparel can make all the difference between a comfortable, enjoyable workout and one that's miserable because of blisters, chafing or dampness. Always opt for comfort over style. There's no need to spend a fortune on designer stuff with logos all over the place.

Wear layers

Being nice and toasty at the beginning of a workout means you're overdressed. You'll be hot and sweaty in no time, and later wet, cold and maybe dehydrated, too. This is why marathon runners compete in close to freezing conditions in nothing more than shorts and singlets. Wear layers so you can ditch them as things heat up.

Choose materials that 'breathe'

Clothing should allow heat and sweat to evaporate, wicking moisture away from the skin. Look for synthetics specially designed for this purpose, or a synthetic/cotton blend. Clothing that is made of 100 per cent cotton is fine for easy workouts in which you don't sweat much, or for top layers that can be shed. Otherwise, avoid having it next to the skin, as it soaks water up like a sponge.

Don't experiment on hard workout days

Avoid experimenting with new shoes and new clothes on hard workout days. Wear stuff that's well broken in, especially if you're competing in a race.

Footwear

A pair of well-built, supportive running shoes will be great for running, walking, group aerobics classes and using fixed exercise machines. If you plan to do several different activities a cross-trainer shoe might be an even better option. Be prepared to spend at least £50 – anything less tends to be poorly constructed or lack decent support. It's a good investment and may save you later pain and visits to the doctor.

Shoes from specialist shops

Shops that specialise in running shoes offer the best selection and consultants to guide you through the mind-boggling assortment of options out there. Take the shoes for a test jog right there in the store; a good store will encourage this sort of thing. If the shoes slide or pinch or feel weird on a little test jog, they'll make you truly miserable after 30 minutes of exercise!

Stick with the shoes you like

Once you find a brand and style you like, stick with it. Save money on future shoes by ordering online or through wholesalers. Be sure to replace shoes often enough – when the rubber treads on the soles start to look worn and smooth or the fabric uppers start ripping, it's time for a fresh pair.

Practical advice: where and when to work out

Your options may be limited, depending on the exercise you do. Swimmers need a large pool or open water; cyclists need long, traffic-free stretches of road; users of fixed exercise equipment usually need to belong to a health club or gym.

Location, location, location

Walkers and runners have the most flexibility when it comes to locations to work out. All they need are a road or trail or track and a good pair of shoes. For those doing the aerobic base programme (and for all beginning exercisers), the ideal training surface is smooth and flat. More advanced walkers, runners and cyclists can incorporate more varied terrain into their workouts, such as hills, steep grades or rough mountain trails. I.T. workouts can be done anywhere, but a measured area is best, such as a track or a footpath with mile markers. Experiment with new places on easy workout days but stick with the tried and true for more challenging workouts. Psychologically, it's easier to work hard in a familiar environment, where you know things like exactly how far there is to go and how long it takes to get to the next turn. On days when the weather is bad or it's too inconvenient to drive to your favourite workout spot, exercising indoors on a treadmill or other machine may be your best bet.

Working out indoors

If you plan to work out indoors with a stair climber, stationary bike, treadmill, or elliptical trainer, you'll most likely have to work out at a gym. Even if you're considering buying a piece of equipment for use at home, it's a good idea to test drive it for a few weeks at a gym before forking out. Some tips for finding a good gym to join:

- Is it close to home or work?
- Does it have lots of aerobic exercise machines? Are they usually occupied at the time of day you want to use them?
- Is there a time limit on machine use? Many gyms have a 20 or 30 minute limit on machines during peak hours. You'll eventually get on, but you may have to interrupt a longer workout session until another machine becomes available.
- Is there good air circulation? Some gyms keep the aerobic area as warm as the weight lifting area. This isn't a good idea, as it can lead to overheating.
- Are the contract terms favourable? Do you have to lock-in to a long-term commitment? Can you use the membership at other clubs?
- Can you get a free pass to try out the place for a few days before signing on the dotted line?
- What's involved in getting out of the contract? You might decide later to join a different gym or take up an outdoor activity instead.

Pushed for time?

Who isn't pushed for time? Unless you have Olympic aspirations or a generous trust fund, it won't always be easy to find time to squeeze in a workout. But with a little sacrifice and creativity, it's entirely possible to find 30 to 60 minutes four to six days a week to improve your fitness, if you really want to.

Exercising consistently requires a good dose of realism. Are you a morning person or a night person? When do you have the most energy, and the least? Can you find an hour before work? On your lunch break? After lectures? Figure out a schedule you can stick to and don't procrastinate when exercise time rolls around – the longer you stall, the harder it is to get out of the door. Sometimes just putting your shoes or swimsuit on is the hardest thing about working out – once you make that mental commitment, it's simply a matter of following through. Or, at least that's what we keep telling ourselves. For some strange reason, it usually works.

No matter how committed you are, though, there are days you just can't work out. You might be sick or travelling or tied up with a huge project at work. Other times your body and mind may shut down and force you to take a day off, despite all your best intentions. Let it happen and don't cave into guilt or try to overcompensate at your next workout. If you find yourself skipping more and more workouts for no apparent reason, you might be pushing too hard physically or have a problem with motivation. Step back, re-evaluate what you're doing, and move on from there.

Special considerations for women

Personal safety

For personal safety, stay aware of your surroundings whenever exercising outdoors. Leave the headphones at home so you can hear if someone is behind you, and try not to be out alone after dark or in remote or deserted areas. Stick to well-lighted, familiar routes and do whatever you can to avoid looking vulnerable, lost or anxious.

Fertility problems

Some female athletes are concerned that intense exercise will cause fertility problems. Interval training can cause some women to have more menstrual irregularities or temporary disruptions in their periods. Some of these disruptions include the rather well-publicised **amenorrhea** (no menstruation), as well as a shortened luteal phase and reduced ovulation, any of which can make getting pregnant more difficult. In simple terms, the added physical stress that a rigorous workout places on the body causes it to shift into an energy-saving mode. This diverts energy from reproductive functions to be available for exercise instead. The result? A skipped menstrual cycle here or there or the absence of a period altogether.

If you're trying to get pregnant, don't worry. In most cases, all that's needed to get a regular cycle going again is to ease up on your training – it's not necessary to stop completely – and make sure you're eating enough. Try backing off on at least one of your more intense workouts each week and eat an extra snack or two, about 300 to 400 calories worth. Chronically missed periods can cause bone mass to decline and lead to stress fractures and osteoporosis, so see your doctor to rule out other problems and to get your periods back on schedule again.

Exercising while pregnant

If you don't have any high-risk conditions and it's okay with your doctor, you don't have to give up exercise while pregnant. On the contrary, studies show that exercising while pregnant has many benefits: active women seem to have calmer babies, fewer complications, shorter labour and deliveries, and are less likely to develop gestational diabetes or other problems. It helps get your pre-baby body back more quickly after delivery, too, and that's certainly a plus. But save the intense training of the I.T. programme for after the baby arrives. Pregnancy puts enough stress on the body as it is, and topping it off with a demanding exercise programme may be harmful to the developing baby. Stick to moderate exercise only during pregnancy and avoid fatigue, heat and dehydration. Be sure to consult your doctor immediately if you experience any faintness, pain, absence of foetal movement, sudden swelling or a racing heart during or after a workout. It may be nothing, but it's best to play it safe for the full nine months.

Special considerations for teenagers

Diet

It takes a lot of energy to be a teenager and even more to be a teenage athlete. Diet is especially important for teens, as they need more calories and nutrients than people at any other stage of life. The average 11 to 14 year old boy needs at least 2500 calories a day, and boys 15 and older need about 2800. Add 1000 calories or so on top of that for those playing sports or training with the I.T. programme. Girls need at least 2200 calories a day, plus an additional 800 if they are doing a lot of exercise. That's a serious amount of food, and any parent of a teenage athlete probably has the grocery bills to prove it.

The majority of these calories should not come from junk food. Teenagers should take healthy snacks to school to have throughout the day and should eat a variety of foods. Dairy products are good sources of calcium, which is especially important for teenagers who are still growing bone. Of course, every teenager we know would much rather have a fizzy soft drink than a carton of milk, but building up bone mass during adolescence can help prevent exercise-related problems later on in life. So keep nagging.

I.T. and the teenage athlete

With some common sense, the I.T. programme can be used safely and to great effect by teenagers, and school swimming and running programmes already use similar training techniques. Adolescents do need to be especially cautious of overuse injuries, poor coaching, improper technique, pushing beyond simple fatigue, and participating in unhealthy forms of competition. If you are a concerned parent or guardian, here are some points to consider if your teen is in an athletic training programme:

• Teenagers are not small adults. Some aches and pains are expected for every athlete, but a teenager's complaints should be given extra-careful consideration. Undiagnosed, untreated injuries can cause permanent damage to developing bones, muscles, tendons, and ligaments and can impede proper growth. Never allow a teen to work 'through the pain'.

• Encourage flexibility and strength training so teens can better maintain muscle balance and suppleness. The joggers you see today who can barely touch their shins (much less their toes) began losing this ability in high school. Start good habits early to avoid overuse injuries later on in life.

• Young athletes of the same age can differ greatly in size and physical maturity and may try to perform at levels they're not ready for.

• Teens are more likely than adults to become overheated and develop heat-related illness. Vigorous activity on very hot days should be limited to early morning or late afternoon (preferably after sunset) when temperatures are cooler, and teenage athletes should be encouraged to drink lots of fluids.

• Teenage athletes need proper guidance and training, and that means qualified coaching. Often schools and sports clubs make their own hiring decisions and parents have little say in the matter. But talk to other parents and observe a few workouts to see if the coach teaches proper technique and keeps workouts to a reasonable level of difficulty. A good coach tailors workouts to each athlete's ability and knows when enough is enough.

• Teenagers should be allowed to explore a variety of athletic activities. Whatever sport they choose, foster an atmosphere of healthy competition that stresses self-reliance, confidence, cooperation and positive self-image over winning at all costs.

Considerations for older exercisers

Most active people intend to continue exercising for the rest of their lives. And these days it's truly possible—people are living longer, healthier lives, practising good preventative care, benefiting from the advances of modern medicine and working out at ages thought unimaginable years ago. The I.T. programme is not designed for the frail elderly, but for healthy individuals; it can have a positive impact on many common geriatric problems: it can reduce and prevent muscle weakness, decreased muscle mass, low bone density, cardiovascular deconditioning, and poor balance. If you play it smart and maximise what you have, there's no reason why you shouldn't be able to keep on using the I.T. programme far past your retirement party. Here are some specific considerations for older exercisers to keep in mind:

- Aerobic capacity declines after the ripe old age of 30, but it's possible to slow the slide. An active middle-aged person can be more physically fit than a university-aged couch potato, so it's worthwhile to make exercise a lifelong habit. Anaerobic capacity declines at an even faster rate, but that's usually because people do less high-intensity exercise as they age. Keeping up your I.T. workouts will hold losses to a minimum.

- The older you get, the longer it takes to recover from workouts. You can't really overcome this, unfortunately – you just have to learn to accommodate it. After a tough workout or a race, give yourself enough time to fully rest before the next hard effort. You may need to incorporate more active rest days into your I.T. programme.

- Joints get stiffer and muscles becomes less flexible with time, so buckle down and start stretching on a regular basis.

- It's easier to gain fat and lose muscle mass with age. Metabolism slows by about 5 per cent every 10 years, and strength, speed and stamina start to dwindle along with bone tissue. It's just a part of life, but you can do a lot to stave off these changes by adding strength training to your exercise programme.

- For active people, particularly competitive athletes, it can be hard to keep up motivation as the years go by. Priorities change, you can't train as hard and you have more injuries or nagging aches and pains. But try to remember that a good exercise programme keeps you healthier and active far longer than retreating to your rocking chair ever will. Some older athletes actually get a kick out of competing in higher age brackets because they come away with more trophies and fanfare than they ever managed in their salad days. A good attitude and a sense of humour are key if you want to keep making the most out of your body and your life.

Older people do have more sports-related injuries, many stemming from years of athletic wear and tear and age-related changes that make tissues more prone to injury. But that's no reason to stop exercising; just take a few extra precautions:

- Follow the medical precaution guidelines outlined earlier in this chapter.

- Make sure your programme includes cardiovascular work, strength training, and flexibility exercises.

- Pay attention to symptoms. If you ever have pain in your chest, left arm, jaw, or upper back, or severe shortness of breath or faintness, see your doctor immediately.

- Pay attention to pain, especially if it's in your joints. See a doctor right away if the pain is only on one side or doesn't go away after a day or two. Also, take more active rest days and allow yourself at least one full day off each week.

③ Your first I.T. workout

Interval training is a whole different animal from purely aerobic exercise. In fact, an alternate title for this book could very well be *Anaerobics*, as the goal of an I.T. workout is to fatigue the body with brief periods of higher intensity effort. This greater level of effort triggers biochemical, cardiovascular, and muscular changes to create a fitter, leaner body. The result: maximum gain, the most efficient way possible.

A firm grasp of the building blocks that form the I.T. workout will help you get the most out of training. Some terms used throughout this book are explained below.

Repetition (rep)

A repetition is the high-intensity portion of an I.T. workout, a period of greater exertion lasting from 30 seconds to about five minutes. Depending on how challenging you want your workout to be and how much time you have, you do a certain number of repetitions with a lower-intensity rest interval between each one. For example, a runner might run eight fast repetitions of 400 metres (one lap around a regulation-size track), with intervals of 200 metres (half a lap) of slow jogging in between each rep.

A repetition is measured by distance or by time. Any predetermined distance, such as 400 metres, can be used. This method obviously works best in a measured setting where exact distances can be easily monitored, such as a standard track, a standard size swimming pool, or a stationary bicycle or treadmill with an electronic mileage function.

Measuring a repetition by time is just as effective and is more flexible in terms of where it can be done. For instance, a cyclist might do five repetitions in a high gear, each lasting two minutes, with three minute intervals in a much lower gear to recover between reps. Use a stopwatch when it's hard to judge exact distances, such as on a footpath without clear mile measurements or when using a stair climber.

Keeping track of the number of repetitions you manage to complete during each I.T. workout is an easy way to chart progress and see how much your conditioning is improving.

Interval (rest)

An interval is the recovery period between the more strenuous repetitions and is also measured by distance or by time. It's called 'interval training' and not 'repetition training' for good reason: the interval determines how much rest the body gets between repetitions, and that greatly influences the intensity of each rep. For instance, if the interval between one minute runs is 10 minutes long, there's ample time to rest and prepare to run the next rep very fast. But if there's only 30 seconds to rest, running that next rep at the same fast pace is a much bigger challenge. Intervals are usually done as 'active rest', such as slow walking or jogging; this actually speeds the clearance of lactic acid better than resting at a complete standstill does. A possible exception to this is swimming in a pool in which lanes are assigned according to speed. In this case, the interval may be a rest at the nearest wall so as not to hinder other swimmers.

Intensity

Intensity is the degree of effort used to complete a repetition and can be determined several ways.

Time

Covering a certain distance in a specific amount of time, such as swimming 50 metres in one minute.

Level

Graduated steps of effort electronically programmed into certain fixed exercise machines. For example, doing a two minute repetition on a stair climber at level eight, followed by a two minute interval at an easier, lower level.

Pulse – Heart rate during or immediately after completing a repetition. Accurate readings during exercise require a heart rate monitor, which for most people is an unnecessary expense (see pages 24–5).

Subjective assessment (or 'feel')

This rather hard to define gauge of intensity is commonly used by advanced-level athletes. With some experience, it can be a very useful method.

How do all these elements – repetitions, intervals, intensity – come together? Some practical examples might help. Here's how an I.T. workout for a stair climber might look jotted down on paper:

5 x 1 minute at level 8/2 minutes at level 4

Translation? The first half refers to the repetition: five high intensity one minute reps on level eight. The other half refers to the interval: two minutes of active rest done at the easier level four between the repetitions.

Here's an example using distance instead of time. A world-class distance runner who wants to run six 1 mile repetitions at a four and a half minutes per mile pace might have a workout that looks like this:

6 x 1 mile in 4:30/¼ mile jog

By manipulating repetition length, repetition number, level of intensity, and interval length, you can easily design I.T. workouts using combinations as infinite as the imagination. Adjust things up or down depending on your level of conditioning, how strong or tired you feel, how much time you have to exercise and so forth.

Ready to give I.T. a try?

With interval training, it's always better to take a few minutes to think through the workout before starting. Here's how to go about it, step by step.

Determine total I.T. time or distance

To figure out how much of a workout should actually be devoted to I.T., just take your total workout time, subtract the time needed for warm-up and cooldown, and use the remaining time for I.T. For instance, for someone who usually exercises on a stair climber for 30 minutes at level three, an I.T. workout might be broken down like this:

10 minute warm-up
15 minutes of interval training (repetitions followed by intervals)
5 minute cooldown
Total: 30 minutes

For a swimmer who swims 40 lengths daily, a first I.T. workout might be:

10 lengths warm-up
24 lengths of I.T.
5 lengths cooldown
Total: 39 lengths

Warm-up and cooldown

It's a good idea to adequately warm up and cool down whenever doing interval training. Because I.T. workouts are done at a higher intensity, it's important for muscles to be warm and supple before starting. A brief warm-up kicks fuel stores into gear, lessens the chance of injury, and maximises the quality of the workout. Elite athletes sometimes spend up to 45 minutes warming up before a challenging session, but five to 15 minutes of activity at a slow pace is fine for most people. For example, a runner planning a three mile or 30 minute I.T. workout might warm up with a one mile (10 minute) jog. Afterward, a slow five to 10 minute cooldown lets the body gradually return to its pre-exercise state, helping speed recovery between workouts.

Choose either time or distance

If you exercise in a measured setting, such as a track or a lap pool or on a bike with an odometer function, it's easy to use specific distances. Otherwise, you'll want to go by time, which can be used in any environment.

One minute reps, two minute intervals

There are good reasons for starting off with one minute repetitions and two minute intervals, and they will be discussed in more detail later. For now, keep it simple and fit as many sets of one minute repetitions and two minute intervals as you can into the workout time you have. For the stair climber example above, the I.T. portion of the workout is broken down like this:

10 minute warm-up at low intensity
five repetitions of one minute at a higher level, with two minute intervals
    at a lower level between reps
five minute cooldown at low intensity
Total: 30 minutes

The same ratio works for distance-based workouts, too, although there's a bit more estimating that needs to be done. For instance, if it normally takes 75 seconds to run half a lap around a track at your baseline aerobic exercise pace, do half a lap for your repetition distance as well (since you'll run it at a faster pace, it will take closer to 60 seconds to complete the same distance). The same thing goes for estimating interval distances. If it usually takes 90 seconds to swim one length at your baseline aerobic exercise pace, use one length as the distance for your I.T. intervals (intervals are done at an even slower pace, so the one length will take closer to two minutes to complete). Rounding off a bit is perfectly okay.

A swimmer who normally swims 90 second lengths will have a first I.T. workout that looks like this:

10 length warm-up at a slow pace
12 repetitions of one length at a higher intensity, with slower one length
    intervals between reps (this assumes that you can swim both fast and
    slow in a given lane; otherwise, spend two minutes at the wall between
    reps)
five length cooldown at a slow pace
Total: 39 lengths

Step up/step down to determine intensity

Figuring out just how hard to push yourself is one of the more challenging aspects of the I.T. programme, so the best strategy is to keep things simple. Intensity can be measured numerous ways, but when you're just starting out, it's a good idea to go with the step up/step down method.

Step up/step down is just what it says: after warming up, step up the intensity one notch from your baseline aerobic workout pace for repetitions, and step down one level from baseline pace for the intervals. Here are a few examples to illustrate how it works:

Walking

Briefly warm up at an easy walking pace, then jog the repetitions (a step up in intensity) and walk slowly for the intervals (a step down in intensity).

What does an I.T. workout feel like?

Unlike the steady pace of an aerobic workout, in which you feel pretty comfortable throughout, an I.T. workout entails a seesaw of fatigue and recovery that may be a tad hard to get used to at first. That first hard repetition is likely to be much more difficult than you imagined. Don't worry – your larger muscle fibres are just protesting as they shift into full work mode, and things generally smooth out by the second and third repetitions. Your mission is to maintain the same level of intensity for each rep you do, which isn't as easy as it sounds.

As an I.T. workout progresses, the repetitions will feel like they're getting harder and the intervals will feel shorter and shorter. Just remember that the benefit of this workout comes when you are tired, not when it's easy! Strangely enough, you may experience a sort of second wind towards the end of your workout and feel an urge to increase the intensity of the repetitions. Try to avoid doing this and focus instead on finishing feeling strong. You can always make adjustments to your next workout.

Running
Warm up with a slow run, then stride out – a fast pace, but not as fast as full-out sprinting – during the rep (a step up in intensity) and jog the intervals (a step down in intensity).

Swimming
Warm up by swimming several easy lengths, then increase the stroke rate so each repetition is about 10 to 30 per cent faster than your baseline aerobic exercise pace (a step up in intensity). For the intervals, decrease the stroke rate to 20 to 40 per cent below your baseline aerobic pace (a step down in intensity).

Cycling
Warm up with some easy spinning in your usual gear, then shift two to three gears higher for the reps. Shift down two or three gears below your baseline gear for the intervals.*

Fixed exercise machines
Warm up at a low level of resistance, then, for the repetitions, increase the effort level so it's about 20 to 40 per cent harder than your baseline aerobic exercise pace (a step up in intensity). For instance, if you normally cruise at level four, do the reps at level five or six. For the intervals, decrease the effort level about 20 to 50 per cent below your baseline aerobic pace (a step down in intensity). Again, if your usual level is four, try level two or three for the interval.*

*Note: Be sure to keep the turnover (the number and depth of steps for stair climbers, rpms for bikes, strokes per minute for rowing machines) at the same level as in your baseline aerobic workout. Otherwise, it's easy to cheat by going slower.

Remember, these are just guidelines. Precise intensity levels aren't of such great importance for your first I.T. workout. Instead, focus on getting used to alternating levels of hard and easy exercise.

Once you finish

Most people come to the same conclusion after they finish their first I.T. workout:

It's tiring!

I.T. is definitely more physically challenging than the moderate aerobic exercise that most people do for each and every workout session. Any physical activity is better than nothing, of course, but for those who are dedicated to achieving greater fitness in less time, a leisurely stroll with a book on a treadmill just isn't going to cut it.

Why you don't need a heart rate monitor

With the I.T. programme, you don't need to invest in an expensive heart rate monitor (or do complicated mathematical formulas to figure out target training zones or anything like that). The manufacturers tout these monitors as crucial pieces of equipment, particularly for beginning exercisers, who

First I.T. workout checklist

- **Warm-up**: Do at least five minutes (preferably 10) at a slightly lower intensity than your baseline aerobic exercise pace

- **Repetition**: Go one minute (or equivalent distance) at a step up from baseline aerobic exercise pace

- **Interval**: Go two minutes (or equivalent distance) at a step down from baseline aerobic exercise pace

- **Repeat**: One one minute repetition/two minute interval cycle as many times as the I.T. portion of your workout allows (I.T. portion = your baseline aerobic exercise workout time, minus warm-up and cooldown time)

- **Cooldown**: Continue exercising for at least five minutes at a very low intensity level tend to overdo things in the first few weeks. But different people have different heart rate tolerances during workouts. For instance, a world-class runner can sustain 80 to 90 per cent of his maximum heart rate for the 2+ hours it takes to finish a marathon. A novice runner can handle such a high rate for only a few minutes. So which runner should be training at 80 per cent of his maximum heart rate? The heart might pump oxygenated blood like crazy, but that doesn't mean the muscles can use that oxygen effectively. Heart rate also fluctuates with temperature, stress, dehydration and lack of sleep, so it's a complicated indicator. If you aren't sure how to interpret it, a heart rate monitor won't do you much good.

Is it possible for an inexperienced exerciser, or any non-elite athlete, to intuitively work out at an appropriate intensity without a heart rate monitor? Certainly. The I.T. programme helps you gain more experience listening to your own body, so you'll know how it feels to be exercising at an optimal training rate. Of course, if you need to be extra cautious due to health problems (if you have heart disease, for example, or high blood pressure), a heart rate monitor might very well be a useful tool to have on hand. Check it out with your doctor.

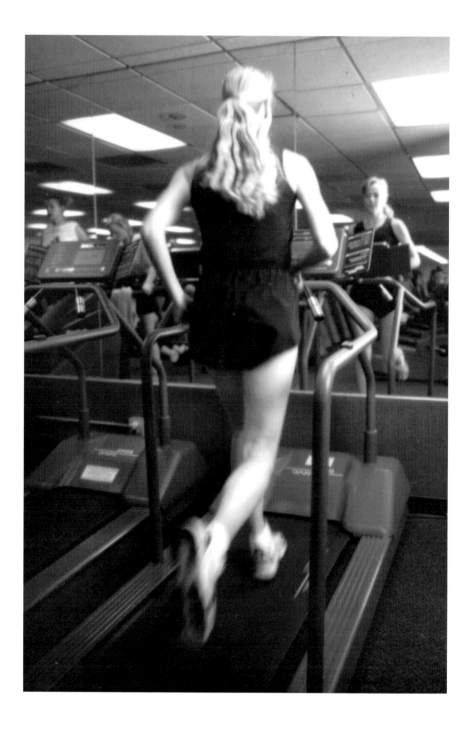

④ Customising your I.T. workout

The beauty of the I.T. programme is in being able to adjust any of the four variables – number of repetitions, length of repetitions, interval length, and intensity – for a full range of training options, from easy to ultra-demanding.

Of course, this flexibility can also be a curse. Having too many choices leaves some people with option paralysis, like kids in a sweet shop flummoxed by a huge display of lollipops. But knowing how and when to change each variable of the I.T. programme is crucial to making headway towards your fitness goals. Develop a starting point – an optimal I.T. workout – then experiment a bit, customising your workout one adjustment at a time. Your I.T. workout is a work in progress, slowly evolving as your fitness improves.

Developing an optimal I.T. workout

Before you start customising an optimal I.T. workout for yourself, think back to how you felt after your first I.T. workout.

Were you too tired to complete the workout?

Be honest: were you too tired to complete the workout? Or, did you finish but feel like a piece of overcooked hamburger by the end? That's okay; it happens sometimes. You're learning your limitations, so just think of it as a subtle clue that the intensity level needs adjusting. It's easy to fall into the 'more is better' trap and take two steps up instead of just one. If you planned to do 10 reps but could only finish eight, chances are you were just pushing too hard and need to scale back the intensity next time. Another thing to consider is your level of fitness. Be honest: have you overestimated your fitness level? Are you truly ready for interval training? If not, don't sweat it. Just stick to aerobic exercise for another month or so, slowly increasing the intensity or the distance covered, and then move on to the more challenging I.T. workouts. Your body will thank you for it.

Did you complete your workout with ease?

If you completed your first I.T. workout with ease, it means you didn't work hard enough! That's okay – it's not a bad idea to be on the conservative side when first starting out. Next time, nudge the intensity up a bit. Remember, it's those spikes in effort that enhance the I.T. effect, provided you don't cheat by compensating with fewer reps, shorter reps or longer recovery intervals. Keep making adjustments until you have an optimal I.T. workout – this usually takes from two to four sessions.

Did you finish tired but able to do more if you had to?

This is the optimal I.T. workout, exactly how you want to feel after a hard training session.

Once you have achieved that perfectly balanced, fatiguing-but-not-exhausting I.T. workout, it's time to shake things up and change it.

Huh? Why mess with success?

The thing is, the body doesn't improve without change – it adapts to whatever physical stress is heaped upon it, which is why the same workout that used to be so tough can eventually be done with greater ease. The ante needs to be upped again and again for progress to continue. Here's how to manipulate the four variables to make a stronger impact with your I.T. workout.

Intensity

The intensity of each repetition is the first variable to adjust. The step up/one step method is an easy way for beginners to determine how much to increase or decrease the effort level, but there are other ways to do it, too.

Level

Level is useful with fixed exercise machines, such as treadmills, stationary bicycles, or stair climbers. Being able to crank up the level of resistance is a sure indicator of improved fitness.

Time

Time is a method that works best when the repetition is an unvarying, measurable distance, such as once around a track or a lap in the pool. Your ability to go at a progressively faster pace, completing each rep in less time, means your physical conditioning is getting better and better.

Feel

Feel is less black and white than other methods of gauging intensity, but it's the most flexible way and the one used most by elite athletes. You already use feel to some degree during your I.T. workouts when you aim to finish up feeling tired but able to do a few more repetitions if you had to. Think of a runner doing repetitions at a stride pace. After doing enough interval training, she knows her abilities and can tell if she's running easy or hard. Being able to run more hard strides means she's improved her level of conditioning.

Self-assessment can be made less vague by using a number scale. You might say you did a rep at a 'seven out of 10' pace, with one being very easy and 10 being your maximum effort. Or use a short word description to describe it, just as Joe Douglas, famed coach of the US Santa Monica Track Club, uses with his runners: 'easy' is a jog; '25 per cent' is an average, natural pace; 'fresh' is as fast as you can go while still able to hold a conversation; 'good' is fast enough to cause fatigue; and 'hard' is just short of going all out. Granted, 'fresh' for a nationally ranked distance runner is going to be quite different than 'fresh' for a 15 mile a week jogger, but it doesn't matter. Feel can take some getting used to, so experiment with it by recording the intensity of your reps in a training log, using whatever means of description works best for you.

Repetition number

Once you have a better sense of how hard to push yourself, the next adjustment should be to the number of repetitions you do. This is the easiest variable of all to adjust – doing more reps is tougher than doing fewer, right? This is generally true – as long as each repetition is done at the same intensity, that is!

It's actually a good thing if you have only a limited amount of time to devote to each I.T. workout. The body can only do so many quality repetitions before fatigue sets in. Push past fatigue and eventually the intensity level starts to free-fall and form gets sloppy (which increases the risk of injury). Pretty soon the whole workout is as flat as a purely aerobic workout, without the distinctive peaks and valleys of interval training. This defeats the whole purpose of the I.T. workout, the goal of which is to become more fit in less time. For this reason, the core I.T. workouts (outlined later in this book) generally limit the number of repetitions to no more than 50 to 60 per cent more than in your baseline aerobic workout. Quality over quantity is always best for this particular workout.

If you're too wiped out to finish all the reps you planned to do, at least try to 'put in the time' and finish what's left of your workout at a slow, easy pace. Next time, do fewer reps and let your body fully adjust before adding any more. If things are too easy, try doing more repetitions next time.

Whatever you do, don't make the mistake of skipping the warm-up and cooldown in order to cram more reps into an I.T. workout. The warm-up and cooldown go far in terms of injury prevention, and the handful of minutes it takes can avert future pain and wasted recovery time. Don't sacrifice your health just to get in a few more reps.

Repetition length

A repetition length of one minute (or a roughly equal distance) is a good starting point for three reasons:

- One minute of intense (but less than maximum effort) exercise uses approximately 50 per cent aerobic and 50 per cent anaerobic energy.
- One minute is long enough to get into a rhythm at a certain pace, without feeling as if you're constantly starting and stopping.
- One minute is short enough to concentrate on sustaining a particular level of effort (something that gets harder with fatigue).

When should you change the length of your repetitions? When you are trying to meet specific goals.

Longer repetitions (more than one minute and done at a slightly lower intensity) require more aerobic and less anaerobic energy to complete. They develop stamina—the ability to go faster for a longer distance or time. Shorter repetitions (about 30 seconds or so) are more anaerobic because they can be done at a higher level of effort. Shorter reps increase muscle power by developing more large muscle fibres, which come in handy when you're trying to beat your cycling buddies to the top of a steep hill.

You can also change repetition length whenever you want to add more spice to your workouts. Try mixing it up, doing long repetitions one session and short reps the next, to give your body better overall physical stamina and conditioning.

Interval

For most people, a rest interval of two minutes between one minute repetitions is ideal. It's long enough for lactic acid to clear out, yet not so long that muscles get overly cool (and thus more prone to injury). Remember, the interval largely dictates the intensity of the repetitions, so altering it can make an I.T. workout geared more for stamina or for speed.

Basically, a shorter interval (one part repetition to one part interval) develops stamina, or aerobic power. Trying to complete high intensity reps with a short recovery period means that a fair amount of lactic acid will still be hanging around, so you'll be working hard in an already fatigued state. That's good training for future competitions, especially those lasting less than 30 minutes. A longer interval (one part repetition to three parts interval) is best for those who want to do ultra-intense repetitions, because there's more time to rest and recover in between. This is the best way to develop the speed you'll need for that final, victorious sprint towards the finish line.

5 Putting it all together: the workouts

The I.T. programme uses a mix of three primary workouts:

- I.T. workouts
- XL workouts
- Active rest days

We will take a closer look at each one of these workouts and at ways to put them all together to create a challenging, results-oriented programme tailored especially for you. At the end of this chapter are complete sample training regimes that incorporate these workouts for optimal fitness.

I.T. workouts

After all this talk about I.T. workouts, you're probably wondering: How often should I do them?

After much trial and error by athletes and coaches, it seems that doing I.T. workouts twice a week, with at least 48 hours between sessions, provides the best results for most people.

In the 1950s and 1960s, after the track world experienced its initial successes with interval training, an unabashed 'more is better' attitude prevailed. Coaches pushed their athletes through daily (!) I.T. sessions, hoping to attain world-record fitness in world-record time. What they got instead was a bunch of exhausted, injured, and frustrated athletes. Later studies in the '70s and '80s revealed that doing such high intensity exercise too frequently causes hormonal exhaustion. After a certain point the body is no longer able to adapt to the stresses placed upon it, and it basically crashes and burns.

These breakthrough revelations coincided with the 'hard/easy' approach popularised by Bill Bowerman, the famous track coach of the University of Oregon (and one of the founding fathers of Nike). By alternating tough training sessions with easier recovery workouts, Bowerman and his successors produced dozens of world-class distance runners, including Steve Prefontaine. Today, the hard/easy approach is the most widely used method of training for elite athletes everywhere, and it provides the framework for the I.T. programme.

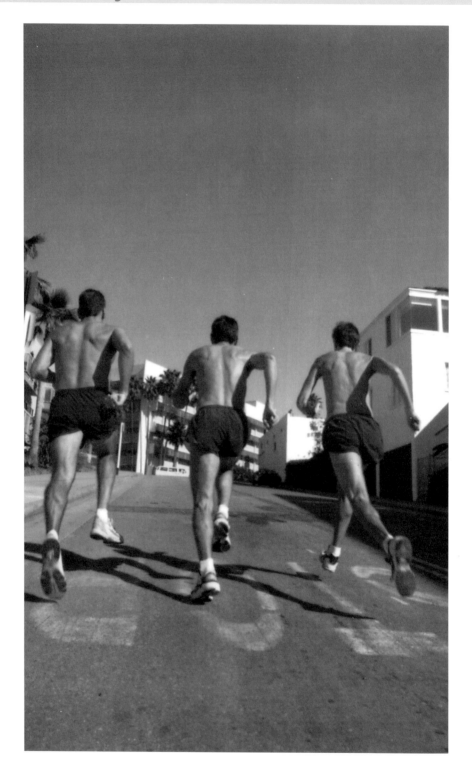

XL workouts

An XL (extra long) workout is simply your baseline aerobic workout done at a comfortable pace for, well, an extra-long time. The XL workout is part of the I.T. programme for two excellent reasons:

• It burns fat

• It builds mitochondria

The longer an aerobic workout lasts, the more fat is used as a source of fuel. At the beginning of an aerobic workout, about two-thirds of the calories you burn are carbohydrates and one-third are fat. As time goes on, however, this ratio slowly changes; an hour into the workout, one-third of the calories burned are carbohydrates and two-thirds are fat. **The longer you go, basically, the more fat you burn**. That's not all. The longer an aerobic workout lasts, the more mitochondria are created. These help muscles use oxygen more efficiently, increasing the amount of exercise you can do aerobically.

Granted, this probably sounds pretty good. That's why some people are happy doing nothing but XL workouts. You've probably seen these types at the gym, magazine in hand, strolling for what seems like forever on the treadmill you're impatiently waiting to use. They must feel they're getting some benefit, otherwise they wouldn't be doing it. But there are drawbacks to doing only this type of exercise. For one thing, it takes a lot of time. It also does nothing in terms of HGH production, it doesn't really work larger muscle fibres, and it doesn't do much to improve the ability to work out or compete at higher intensity levels. In the words of former world record holder and Olympic champion runner Sebastian Coe, 'Long slow distance makes long slow runners.' It's true. XL workouts should be considered as just one element of a successful fitness programme – to get maximum benefits you need to do I.T. workouts and active rest days as well. So limit XL workouts to once a week, ideally at least 48 hours before or after an I.T. workout.

Planning an XL workout is easy. Just do your favourite aerobic exercise for a longer time than usual. Take it somewhat slower, so that you are comfortable and not pushing too hard, and just put in the time. The goal is to gradually increase this workout so that eventually it's one and a half to two times as long (measured by either distance or time) as your I.T. workout, including warm-up and cooldown. For example, if your I.T. workout in the pool takes 30 minutes, build up over time to make your XL workout a slower, steady 45 to 60 minute swim. If you run five miles for your I.T. workout, eventually you'll do 7.5 to 10 miles for your XL session.

An XL workout can be a significant time commitment, no doubt about it. Many people like to schedule these longer sessions on weekends, when they have additional time to exercise. Trust us, it's time well spent. Once you start seeing the tangible results of your I.T. programme, you'll agree that XL workouts are worth the effort.

Active rest days

An 'active rest day' is simply a light exercise session that maintains fitness and increases blood flow to tired muscles, aiding recovery between strenuous I.T. and XL workouts. A good starting point is to do one-half to two-thirds of your baseline aerobic workout at about the same intensity (or slightly slower). If you normally walk on a treadmill for 30 minutes at four mph, for example, try doing 20 minutes at three to four mph on an active rest day. Or use the time to do cross training with a different activity, if that's of interest.

The purpose of active rest is recovery – there's no benefit to making this workout any more challenging than it is. To be perfectly honest, if you can only manage to exercise three days a week, you should use the time for two I.T. workouts and one XL workout (spacing them at least 48 hours apart), and skip the active rest day completely. There will be ample rest the four days you don't work out!

Take a full day off once a week to give your body a break and to let it adapt to the exercise stress. When first starting the I.T. programme, these new, more challenging I.T. and XL workouts may take longer to get used to than you would expect. Be flexible, and add additional active rest days between harder workouts if necessary, or change an active rest day into a full day off from exercise. If the quality of your harder workouts seems to be slipping, or if you feel overly tired or irritable or have trouble sleeping, you're probably pushing your body to do too much. Exercise should make you feel good. It should be fun—you'll never stick with it if it turns into a chore. So, be nice to yourself and don't feel guilty for taking some time off if your body needs more rest.

If you plan to exercise six days a week (which is ideal), the daily breakdown looks like this:

Day 1:	I.T. workout
Day 2:	Active rest day
Day 3:	I.T. workout
Day 4:	Day off
Day 5:	XL workout
Day 6:	Active rest day
Day 7:	Active rest day

Some people use an eight or nine day schedule, giving themselves two active rest days or full days off after each hard workout. This doesn't produce results as quickly, but it's a good plan for older exercisers or those with time or energy constraints. For maximum gains, establish a schedule that works for you within three or four weeks of starting the I.T. programme, and then be consistent with it.

Progressing with the I.T. programme: the first four weeks

Use the first month of the programme to get used to the higher level of intensity. If it feels like the workouts are too hard or you have trouble completing them (even at a slightly slower pace), take an additional active rest day or a full day off, and back off on the effort of your next I.T. workout. If this doesn't resolve the situation, read the section on overtraining in the next chapter.

I.T. workouts

Take a few sessions to figure out your optimal I.T. workout. When it starts to feel easier, slightly increase the repetition intensity. Don't do any additional reps just yet – there's plenty of time for that later.

XL workouts

Keep XL workouts about 25 per cent longer than your baseline aerobic workout. This allows your body to get used to a greater effort without pushing your endurance limits too hard.

Active rest days

On active rest days, do about 50 to 70 per cent of your baseline aerobic workout, at an easier intensity if necessary. The idea is recovery, so if you need to do less at first, by all means do so. Take a full day off at least once a week, two or three if you're still tired from the more strenuous workouts. (If you need more days off than this, tone down the intensity of your next I.T. workout.) No matter how fabulous you feel, don't give in to the temptation to replace easy days with more I.T. and XL workouts – this can lead to too much stress and potential for injury.

Moving forward – week five and beyond

Once you hit week five, it's time to move forward with your I.T. programme. By this time, you should notice that I.T. workouts are getting easier, XL workouts don't seem as long, and active rest days are becoming even more appealing than lazing about the house. Time now to push ahead and further customise your I.T. workouts to meet your individual needs. Here are a few things to keep in mind.

Increase repetition number or repetition intensity

Advance your I.T. workouts by increasing either the repetition number or the repetition intensity. Do one or the other, but never both at the same time! If you increase the number of reps, add only one at a time and keep the upper limit about 50 to 75 per cent above that of your optimal I.T. workout. If you change the intensity, the sky's the limit for how challenging you can make it, but don't go nuts and exhaust yourself. Aim to feel tired but in control at the end of each workout. If you 'hit a wall' with a higher intensity, try doing some reps at your previous intensity and some at the new, higher intensity during the same workout. Then slowly build up in subsequent workouts, doing more and more reps at the higher intensity level.

Change repetition length or interval length

To meet specific goals or to add variety, change the repetition length or the interval length. For example, do one short-rep/long-interval I.T. workout and one long-rep/short-interval workout the same week. Adjusting these variables can be tricky since each one affects intensity, too. Track improvement by keeping notes on repetition number, repetition intensity, and interval length for each I.T. workout you do. As you gain experience, you may want to try some alternative I.T. workouts, such as those discussed at the end of this chapter. These workouts can be a nice break from routine and bring the same physiologic rewards as other I.T. workouts when done with a similar high level of intensity.

Gradually increase the XL workout

Gradually increase the length of your XL workout until it's one and a half to two times as long as the I.T. workout, but no more than two hours. This workout takes considerably more time than the others, but the benefits are great.

Add active rest days whenever you need them

Always feel free to add active rest days whenever you need them. If you start to need too many of these easy days, however, you're pushing too hard and need to adjust your I.T. and XL workouts accordingly.

Don't exercise more than six days a week

Exercising more than six days a week isn't a good idea. Your body needs time to rest and recover from all the physical stress it's being subjected to.

Take an easy week every four to eight weeks

Taking an easy week of active rest days in place of your regular I.T. and XL workouts won't sabotage your fitness – on the contrary, it will let you fully recover and avoid overtraining. Use it to cross train with a different activity if you wish, just for a change of pace. Aim to take an easy week every 4 to 8 weeks. Some people like to schedule these weeks during vacations or holidays, when a normal exercise routine is usually interrupted anyway.

Stay with it

Remember that each workout is a step towards greater fitness. It's not possible to see improvement each and every workout. If it were, we'd all have a box filled with Olympic gold medals. Some days you'll be tired, or just 'off'. It happens to everyone – just do the best you can. If one or two workouts aren't so fabulous, back off a touch on the next session by decreasing either the repetition number or the intensity. If you have several below par workouts in a row, read up on motivation and goal setting in the next chapter. It might help get you out of your rut.

The workouts

These workouts are the specific regimes that make up the I.T. programme. They're based on a seven day cycle and are divided by activity (walking, running, cycling, swimming, and fixed exercise machines) for the first four weeks of the programme and weeks five and beyond.

The I.T. workouts are presented as either 30 minute or 60 minute sessions. If your intended workout time is longer or shorter, make adjustments accordingly.

All I.T. workouts have the same repetition length, repetition number, and interval length for the first four weeks. You'll increase intensity as your fitness improves. In weeks five and beyond, we make recommendations for changing repetition number, intensity, and interval length. *Only adjust one variable at a time (you make the call on which one) and make changes gradually.* Just increase one rep at a time, for example, or slowly raise the intensity level or decrease the interval length over the course of several workouts.

All repetitions and intervals are based on time but can be easily converted to distance if you exercise in a measured setting (such as a track, marked trail, or pool, or if you use an odometer).

Some alternative I.T. workout ideas can be found at the end of this chapter. Once you're past the first four weeks, shake up your programme now and then by substituting one of these workouts in place of an I.T. session. You might even decide to make one or more of these alternative workouts a regular part of your I.T. programme.

Abbreviations used:

WU   =   warm-up (to be done at an easy, comfortable pace)
CD   =   cooldown (also at an easy pace)
I.T. =   interval workout
XL   =   extra-long workout
AR   =   active rest day (performed at intensity recommended or slightly lower intensity)
min =   minute(s)
sec =   second(s)

To make things easier, I.T. workouts are written in this format:

repetition number × repetition length
and intensity/interval time

For instance, eight one minute reps done at level six with a two minute interval at level two is written as:

8 × 1 min at level 6/2 min at level 2

Walking

These schedules are for walkers doing 30 to 60 minutes of exercise four to six times a week. Intensity levels: slow walk, walk (your normal pace), jog and run.

Weeks 1 to 4 – 30 minutes

Day 1:	I.T. WU 10 min 5 × 1 min jog/2 min slow walk CD 5 min
Day 2:	AR 15–20 min walk
Day 3:	I.T. WU 10 min 5 × 1 min jog/2 min slow walk CD 5 min
Day 4:	Day off
Day 5:	XL 37–38 min walk
Day 6:	AR 15–20 min walk
Day 7:	AR 15–20 min walk

Weeks 5 and beyond – 30 minutes

Day 1:	I.T. WU 10 min 5 × 1 min jog/2 min slow walk CD 5 min
Reps:	increase to 8 × 1 min
Intensity:	increase to run
Interval:	decrease to 1 min
Day 2:	AR 15–20 min walk
Day 3:	I.T. WU 5 min 4 × 2.5 min jog/2.5 min slow walk CD 5 min
Reps:	increase to 6 × 2.5 min
Intensity:	increase to run
Interval:	decrease to 1.5 min
Day 4:	Day off
Day 5:	XL increase gradually to 45–60 min walk
Day 6:	AR 15–20 min walk
Day 7:	AR 15–20 min walk

Weeks 1 to 4 – 60 minutes

Day 1:	I.T.
	WU 15–20 min
	10 × 1 min jog/2 min slow walk
	CD 5–10 min
Day 2:	AR 30–40 min walk
Day 3:	I.T.
	WU 15–20 min
	10 × 1 min jog/2 min slow walk
	CD 5–10 min
Day 4:	Day off
Day 5:	XL 75 min walk
Day 6:	AR 30–40 min walk
Day 7:	AR 30–40 min walk

Weeks 5 and beyond – 60 minutes

Day 1:	I.T.
	WU 15–20 min
	10 × 1 min jog/2 min slow walk
	CD 5–10 min
Reps:	increase to 15 × 1 min
Intensity:	increase to run
Interval:	decrease to 1 min
Day 2:	AR 30–40 min walk
Day 3:	I.T.
	WU 10–15 min
	5 × 3 min jog/3 min slow walk
	CD 10 min
Reps:	increase to 8 × 3 min
Intensity:	increase to run
Interval:	decrease to 2 min
Day 4:	Day off
Day 5:	XL increase gradually to 90–120 min walk
Day 6:	AR 30–40 min walk
Day 7:	AR 30–40 min walk

Jogging and running

These workouts are for joggers and runners doing 30 to 60 minutes of continuous exercise four to six days a week. Intensity levels used are walk, jog (your normal pace), run, stride (a fast run), and sprint. If you are a more advanced runner, shift all intensities up a notch (substitute a one minute jog for a one minute walk, a 15 minute run for a 15 minute jog, a two minute stride for a two minute run).

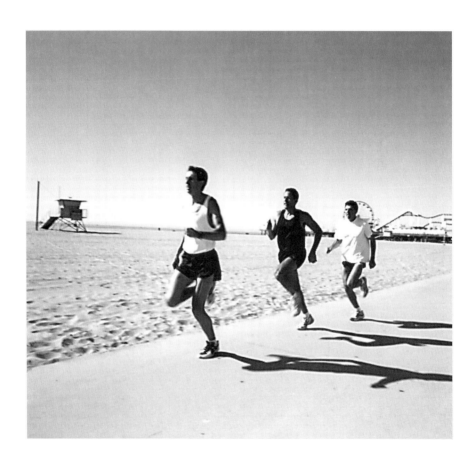

Weeks 1 to 4 – 30 minutes

Day 1:	I.T. WU 10 min 4 × 1 min run/2 min walk CD 5 min
Day 2:	AR 15–20 min jog
Day 3:	I.T. WU 10 min 4 × 1 min run/2 min walk CD 5 min
Day 4:	Day off
Day 5:	XL 37–38 min jog
Day 6:	AR 15–20 min jog
Day 7:	AR 15–20 min jog

Weeks 5 and beyond – 30 minutes

Day 1:	I.T. WU 5 min 4 × 2 min run/3 min walk CD 5 min
Reps:	increase to 7 × 2 min
Intensity:	increase to stride
Interval:	decrease to 2 min
Day 2:	AR 15–20 min jog
Day 3:	I.T. WU 10 min 8 × 30 sec stride/1 min walk CD 5 min
Reps:	increase to 12 × 30 sec
Intensity:	increase to sprint
Interval:	decrease to 45 sec
Day 4:	Day off
Day 5:	XL increase gradually to 45–60 min jog
Day 6:	AR 15–20 min jog
Day 7:	AR 15–20 min jog

Weeks 1 to 4 – 60 minutes

Day 1:	I.T.
	WU 15–20 min
	8 × 1 min run/2 min walk
	CD 5 min
Day 2:	AR 30–40 min jog
Day 3:	I.T.
	WU 15–20 min
	8 × 1 min run/2 min walk
	CD 5 min
Day 4:	Day off
Day 5:	XL 75 min jog
Day 6:	AR 30–40 min jog
Day 7:	AR 30–40 min jog

Weeks 5 and beyond – 60 minutes

Day 1:	I.T.
	WU 15–20 min
	6 × 2 min run/3 min walk
	CD 10 min
Reps:	increase to 8–10 × 2 min
Intensity:	increase to stride
Interval:	decrease to 2 min
Day 2:	AR 30–40 min jog
Day 3:	I.T.
	WU 20 min
	12 × 30 sec stride/1 min walk
	CD 10 min
Reps:	increase to 16–20 × 30 sec
Intensity:	increase to sprint
Interval:	decrease to 45 sec
Day 4:	Day off
Day 5:	XL gradually increase to 90–120 min jog
Day 6:	AR 30–40 min jog
Day 7:	AR 30–40 min jog

Cycling

These workouts are for cyclists who can ride continuously for 30 to 60 minutes in a low to middle gear. Pedalling rate (or rpm) should be kept constant at your natural rhythm. Intensity levels used: low gear, middle gear and high gear. These gear levels are arbitrary; for instance, if you ride a ten-speed bicycle you may normally spin in the fourth gear (low-middle). If this is the case, then second gear will be low gear for you, middle gear may be sixth or seventh, high gear may be ninth or tenth. Adjust accordingly. **Note: Those using stationary bicycles with varying levels of resistance may wish to refer to the fixed exercise machine I.T. programme instead.**

Weeks 1 to 4 – 30 minutes

Day 1:	I.T.
	WU 5 min
	5 × 1 min middle gear/2 min low gear
	CD 5 min
Day 2:	AR 15–20 min low-middle gear
Day 3:	I.T.
	WU 5 min
	5 × 1 min middle gear/2 min low gear
	CD 5 min
Day 4:	Day off
Day 5:	XL 37–38 min low-middle gear
Day 6:	AR 15–20 min low-middle gear
Day 7:	AR 15–20 min low-middle gear

Weeks 5 and beyond – 30 minutes

Day 1:	I.T.
	WU 5 min
	5 × 2 min middle gear/2 min low gear
	CD 5 min
Reps:	increase to 8 × 2 min
Intensity:	increase to high gear
Interval:	decrease to 1.5 min
Day 2:	AR 15–20 min low-middle gear
Day 3:	I.T.
	WU 10 min
	8 × 30 sec high gear/1 min low gear
	CD 5 min
Reps:	increase to 12 × 30 sec
Intensity:	increase to 20 per cent higher rpm in high gear
Interval:	decrease to 45 sec
Day 4:	Day off
Day 5:	XL gradually increase to 45–60 min low-middle gear
Day 6:	AR 15–20 min low-middle gear
Day 7:	AR 15–20 min low-middle gear

Weeks 1 to 4 – 60 minutes

Day 1:	I.T.
	WU 15–20 min
	10 × 1 min middle gear/2 min low gear
	CD 5 min
Day 2:	AR 30–40 min low-middle gear
Day 3:	I.T.
	WU 15–20 min
	10 × 1 min middle gear/2 min low gear
	CD 5 min
Day 4:	Day off
Day 5:	XL 75 min low-middle gear
Day 6:	AR 30–40 min low-middle gear
Day 7:	AR 30–40 min low-middle gear

Weeks 5 and beyond – 60 minutes

Day 1:	I.T.
	WU 15–20 min
	6 × 3 min middle gear/3 min low gear
	CD 5 min
Reps:	increase to 10 × 3 min
Intensity:	increase to high gear
Interval:	decrease to 1.5 min
Day 2:	AR 30–40 min low-middle gear
Day 3:	I.T.
	WU 15–20 min
	12 × 30 sec high gear/1 min low gear
	CD 10 min
Reps:	increase to 20 × 30 sec
Intensity:	increase to 20 per cent higher rpm in high gear
Interval:	decrease to 45 sec
Day 4:	Day off
Day 5:	XL gradually increase to 90–120 min low-middle gear
Day 6:	AR 30–40 min low-middle gear
Day 7:	AR 30–40 min low-middle gear

Swimming

These workouts are designed for swimmers who can do 30 to 60 minutes at a comfortable slow-to-medium pace. Intensity levels used: slow (turnover 20–30 per cent slower than your baseline pace), medium (turnover 10–20 per cent faster than baseline pace), fast (20–30 per cent faster turnover), and sprint (30–40 per cent faster turnover). These are rough estimates – remember that the goal is to finish each intense workout tired, but able to do a bit more if necessary.

There is one minor adjustment that is unique to swimmers: many pools have assigned lanes for various speeds, so varying your intensity during an I.T. workout may not be possible. In this case, swim in the most appropriate lane for your repetition intensity, and spend the interval time resting at the end of the pool. Don't complete more repetitions than recommended. Instead, focus on maintaining a consistent level of intensity, so you are fatigued by the end of the workout.

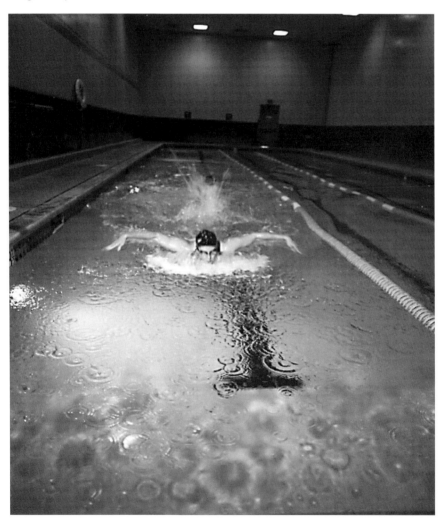

Weeks 1 to 4 – 30 minutes

Day 1:	I.T.
	WU 10 min
	5 × 1 min medium/2 min slow
	CD 5 min
Day 2:	AR 15–20 min slow-medium
Day 3:	I.T.
	WU 10 min
	5 × 1 min medium/2 min slow
	CD 5 min
Day 4:	Day off
Day 5:	XL 37–38 min slow-medium
Day 6:	AR 15–20 min slow-medium
Day 7:	AR 15–20 min slow-medium

Weeks 5 and beyond – 30 minutes

Day 1:	I.T.
	WU 5 min
	4 × 2.5 min medium/2.5 min slow
	CD 5 min
Reps:	increase to 7 x 2.5 min
Intensity:	increase to fast
Interval:	decrease to 1.5 min
Day 2:	AR 15–20 min slow-medium
Day 3:	I.T.
	WU 10 min
	8 × 30 sec fast/1 min slow
	CD 5 min
Reps:	increase to 12 × 30 sec
Intensity:	increase to sprint
Interval:	decrease to 45 sec
Day 4:	Day off
Day 5:	XL gradually increase to 45–60 min slow-medium
Day 6:	AR 15–20 min slow-medium
Day 7:	AR 15–20 min slow-medium

Weeks 1 to 4 – 60 minutes

Day 1:	I.T.
	WU 15–20 min
	10 × 1 min medium/2 min slow
	CD 5–10 min
Day 2:	AR 30–40 min slow-medium
Day 3:	I.T.
	WU 15–20 min
	10 × 1 min medium/2 min slow
	CD 5–10 min
Day 4:	Day off
Day 5:	XL 75 min slow-medium
Day 6:	AR 30–40 min slow-medium
Day 7:	AR 30–40 min slow-medium

Weeks 5 and beyond – 60 minutes

Day 1:	I.T.
	WU 10–15 min
	4 × 5 min medium/3.5 min slow
	CD 5–10 min
Reps:	increase to 7 × 5 min
Intensity:	increase to fast
Interval:	decrease to 2 min
Day 2:	AR 30–40 min slow-medium
Day 3:	I.T.
	WU 20 min
	12 × 30 sec fast/1 min slow
	CD 10 min
Reps:	increase to 20 × 30 sec
Intensity:	increase to sprint
Interval:	decrease to 45 sec
Day 4:	Day off
Day 5:	XL gradually increase to 90–120 min slow-medium
Day 6:	AR 30–40 min slow-medium
Day 7:	AR 30–40 min slow-medium

Fixed exercise machines

These workouts are for exercisers who use stair climbers, stationary bikes, elliptical trainers, and cross-country ski machines for 30 to 60 minutes at a moderate baseline aerobic level four to six days a week. Intensity is measured by this baseline level (referred to here as 'level X'), plus or minus additional levels. Because machine levels are not the same for all types of equipment, you may need to adjust the intensity so that you complete the more intense I.T. and XL workouts tired but feeling like you could do a bit more if necessary. Remember to maintain the same rpm (on cycles, elliptical trainers, and cross-country ski machines) or step rate and depth (on stair climbers) that you would during a normal aerobic workout.

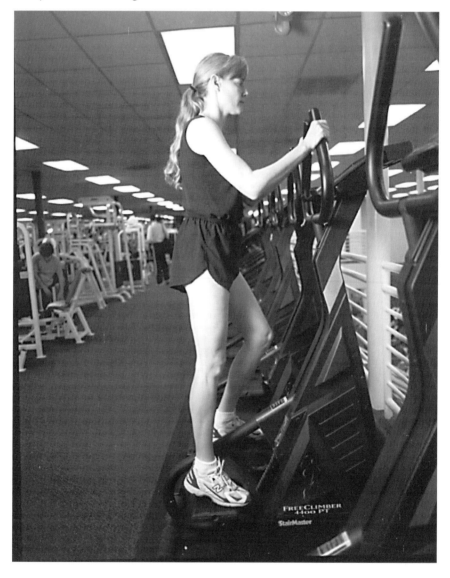

Weeks 1 to 4 – 30 minutes

Day 1:	I.T. WU 10 min 5 × 1 min level X +2/2 min level X –2 CD 5 min
Day 2:	AR 15–20 min level X
Day 3:	I.T. WU 10 min 5 × 1 min level X +2/2 min level X –2 CD 5 min
Day 4:	Day off
Day 5:	XL 37–38 min level X
Day 6:	AR 15–20 min level X
Day 7:	AR 15–20 min level X

Weeks 5 and beyond – 30 minutes

Day 1:	I.T. WU 5 min 4 × 2.5 min level X +2/2.5 min level X –2 CD 5 min
Reps:	increase to 7 × 2.5 min
Intensity:	increase to X +5
Interval:	decrease to 1.5 min
Day 2:	AR 15–20 min level X
Day 3:	I.T. WU 10 min 8 × 30 sec level X +4/1 min level X –2 CD 5 min
Reps:	increase to 12 × 30 sec
Intensity:	increase to X +7
Interval:	decrease to 45 sec
Day 4:	Day off
Day 5:	XL gradually increase to 45–60 min level X
Day 6:	AR 15–20 min level X
Day 7:	AR 15–20 min level X

51

Weeks 1 to 4 – 60 minutes

Day 1:	I.T.
	WU 15–20 min
	8–10 × 1 min level X +2/2 min level X –2
	CD 10 min
Day 2:	AR 30–40 min level X
Day 3:	I.T.
	WU 15–20 min
	8–10 × 1 min level X +2/2 min level X –2
	CD 10 min
Day 4:	Day off
Day 5:	XL 75 min level X
Day 6:	AR 30–40 min level X
Day 7:	AR 30–40 min level X

Weeks 5 and beyond – 60 minutes

Day 1:	I.T.
	WU 20 min
	5 × 3 min level X +2/3 min level X –2
	CD 10 min
Day 2:	AR 30–40 min level X
Day 3:	I.T.
	WU 20 min
	12 × 30 sec level X +4/1 min level X –2
	CD 15 min
Reps:	increase to 20 × 30 sec
Intensity:	increase to X +7
Interval:	decrease to 45 sec
Day 4:	Day off
Day 5:	XL gradually increase to 90–120 min level X
Day 6:	AR 30–40 min level X
Day 7:	AR 30–40 min level X

Alternative I.T. workouts

As you become more familiar with the concept and feel of interval training, you may wish to add a bit more spice to your programme by occasionally doing one or more of the following alternative workouts in place of an I.T. session. These workouts offer an opportunity to learn more about your physical capabilities, and, more importantly, they're fun. Just remember to finish up feeling tired but still able to do a bit more.

Hills

Doing hills (or 'gravity training', as we like to call it) is great for walkers, runners, and cyclists. Do an easy warm-up on the flats, then charge up a moderately steep hill at a good clip for 30 seconds to two minutes, then recover by descending slowly back to the bottom. Do enough of these repetitions and intervals to fill your intended workout time, then do a short cooldown. Another option is to put together a course with several different hills, some short, some long, pushing a bit as you climb to the top and backing off on the way down. If it's too slippery outside, do a hill workout on steps at a stadium or set a treadmill at an incline.

Fartlek

'Fartlek' is a Swedish word that means 'speed play'. It's a fun workout because you get to improvise as you go, doing bursts of speed for different distances with brief rests in between. After warming up, pick a random landmark – a tree some distance away or the end of the block – then just pick up the pace until you get there, slow down for a while to rest, then pick another landmark. It can be done with a stopwatch, too – just speed up for whatever amount of time you decide to do, rest a bit, and repeat. Keep at it until you have only enough gas left to do a little more, then do a short cooldown. Fartlek training can be done with any aerobic exercise, and it's especially useful when you're in unfamiliar surroundings or when easing back into speedwork after taking a little break from the programme.

Group exercise

Using fixed exercise machines – treadmills, stationary bikes, stair climbers – by yourself can get to be a real snooze after a while. But now many gyms offer fun group exercise options such as 'spinning' – a group cycling class guided by a coach who plays music and helps riders visualise things like cruising the plains or surging up a mountain pass in the Tour de France. Try one of these classes to help get you through. And, for any exercise activity, it's never a bad idea to find some training partners. Working out with other people is a great way to stay motivated, especially on hard days, and it helps make the time fly by.

AT (anaerobic threshold) workouts

AT workouts are specifically designed to train your body to manage lactic acid buildup over an extended period of time. After warming up, go for 15 to 20 minutes at a substantially higher level of effort than your baseline aerobic workout. Think of it as a 90 per cent effort – you should be fairly tired two-thirds of the way through, and you should finish feeling like you could go on only if there were a gold medal on the line. Take a moment to catch your breath, then do a short cooldown. This type of workout is really taxing, so pace yourself and do it only occasionally.

Ladders and pyramids

Varying repetition lengths can really jazz up an I.T. workout. Try a 'ladder', doing a five minute rep, then a four minute, then a three minute, and so on, making the interval equally long as each repetition. Or try a 'pyramid': a one minute rep, then a two minute, then a three minute, then a four minute; back down to a three minute, a two minute, and a one minute; again using equally long intervals. Vary the intensity with the repetition length – ease back a bit for the longer reps, go faster for the shorter ones. Remember to warm up and cool down before and after these workouts, too.

Programmed workouts

Many fixed exercise machines such as treadmills and stationary bikes have preprogrammemed workouts that can vary intensity for you. Try to choose programmes with a wide range of intensity levels and work to keep going at the same pace throughout.

Off-road workouts

Off-road workouts are a lot like Fartlek workouts, the idea being to find more difficult terrain (such as a mountain bike trail, a beach, a hilly golf course, or a sea or lake). Outside the controlled environment of a track or a flat road or a pool, the forces of nature conspire against good form and make things extra challenging. Pick up the intensity on the tougher sections – swim harder against the tide, run on the softer sand (where there's less traction and stability), lean hard on the pedals up a muddy trail. As always, work until you can only do a little more, then take an easy cooldown.

6 The mental edge: motivation and goal setting

Millions of people pledge over and over every New Year's Eve to finally buckle down and get into shape. Why can't more people stick with it?

It isn't easy, that's why. In these hectic, over-scheduled times, exercising consistently is a real challenge, especially early in the morning when you're bleary-eyed with sleep or after work when dinner, friends, family and television programmes seem to take priority. Working out may do wonders for your physique and self-esteem and may even make you feel a bit superior to your friends and colleagues (come on, admit it) who can't muster the same discipline. But even the most dedicated competitive athletes peer out at the bleak pre-dawn sky sometimes and wonder why on earth they aren't still snoozing in bed, like all the normal people.

The truth is that exercising regularly is not considered normal by a good portion of the general population. Anyone who has ever worked out early in the morning, or in the pouring rain has no doubt noticed a strange look or two. These tend to be either wistful (envious?) glances or expressions that seem to say, 'I can't believe anyone is mad enough to be out exercising in this.' If you're devoted to attaining peak conditioning or even if you just want to make exercise a daily part of your life, you need to find a reliable way to stay motivated. It's hard, especially when you're exercising on your own, but if you believe enough in what you're doing, you'll somehow manage to crawl out of bed. The benefits of exercise make all the inconveniences worthwhile.

The encouraging thing is that if you've made it this far in this book, you probably already have what it takes to succeed. Nonetheless, your mind and your body may not always be on the same page when it comes to physical fitness, and at those times it helps to have some tricks to kick the two back into sync. Ask yourself the following:

- Are you motivated to work out most of the time, with only a few days a month on which you miss a workout or make a halfhearted effort because you don't feel like exercising?

- Do you find yourself dreading your next workout?

- Do you miss at least one scheduled workout a week?

Exercise should be a lifelong priority, so an occasional lack of willpower or a skipped workout is perfectly fine – even healthy – and nothing to beat yourself up about. What needs to be avoided at all costs is the attitude that not completing a workout somehow screws up all that's been previously

accomplished and that continuing is pointless. This is a silly but remarkably easy mental trap to fall into, and people on diets do it all the time. 'I just blew my whole diet with that chocolate biscuit, so today is a total loss and I may as well eat the rest of the packet.' Obviously, this defies all logic, but it's typical of the tricky nature of motivation. It's a head game, but you are in control. Every athlete at one time or another has substituted a nap or an evening with the remote control for a hard interval workout. Life is unpredictable and success comes through being flexible. So, unless you're training for the Olympic Games, adapt your workout schedule to fit into your life. A day off here and there can give you a much-needed mental and physical break and let you come back with greater energy and enthusiasm next time.

The same thing holds true when you're on holiday or away from home. It's harder to exercise at the same intensity or for the same length of time in unfamiliar surroundings. So relax and enjoy yourself and turn your workouts into an opportunity to explore. Try something different, such as running along the beach or sightseeing by bicycle, doing two-thirds of what you normally do, at the most. Or, schedule a week of active rest days to coincide with your travels. Even if you skip a session or two entirely, it won't throw your fitness programme completely off kilter. Just plan to put in some quality workouts once you return to 'real life'.

Overtraining

If you find yourself dreading your next workout or miss at least one scheduled workout a week, there's a very good chance that you're doing too much. You're overtraining.

Sometimes the problem with motivation has less to do with overcoming guilt and inertia than it does with knowing when to stop exercising. Although we know that it's possible to exercise too much, overtraining is still a poorly understood physical phenomenon. The human mind, when properly motivated, can push the body to incredible lengths: climbing Mount Everest without oxygen; lifting a car to free a trapped person; running a marathon. But human physiology can adapt only so much and only at a given pace – otherwise, we would all be Olympians. This built-in ceiling of adaptability is completely natural; it's the body's way of ensuring it doesn't run itself right into the ground. Take a few moments sometime to watch children at play. They run around and around until they are too tired to do it anymore and then they stop and take a little nap. Unfortunately, hard-driving fitness enthusiasts and athletes often push right through this natural ceiling in pursuit of greater physical gains.

Over the course of a workout or a week of training, this pushing can lead to sore muscles and mild fatigue. This is expected to some degree – even sought after – in the course of the I.T. programme, because it's a sure sign that you're giving your body a thoroughly effective bout of exercise. I.T. and XL workouts are never done on consecutive days because the schedule is designed to allow adequate physical (and mental) recovery between these more difficult sessions. Occasionally, you may overdo a workout and not recover in time for the next tough session – your working muscles might feel too sore or heavy or you might just lack the energy to complete the work. This is all part of learning your own limitations and is easily remedied with an extra day or two of active rest day workouts or a full day off.

There's a big difference, however, between merely overdoing it now and then and overtraining. Overtraining manifests itself in various ways, including:

• chronic fatigue

• lack of interest in working out

• irritability

• difficulty sleeping

• change in appetite

• lingering muscle soreness

A combination of these symptoms over a couple of weeks can lead to a mild case of exercise-induced depression, where the body tries to protect itself and replace depleted energy stores by refusing to adapt to any more physical stress. If you are willing to work towards greater fitness, you can't completely avoid the possibility of overtraining. The line between not enough and too much is extremely fine and changes over time as the body better adapts to stress. Almost everyone who follows a demanding fitness programme and remains injury-free ends up in an exercise funk at some point. But good habits – such as proper diet, getting enough sleep, stretching, strength training and cross training with other activities – can help you better tolerate the tougher workouts and recover from them more quickly.

World-class runners, swimmers, cyclists and others at the highest levels of fitness tend to live like clocks, their daily lives scheduled with almost inhuman regularity – awake at a certain time, workout at a certain time, eat at a certain time, workout, rest, eat, sleep, repeat ad nauseam. Those T-shirts that say 'Eat, Sleep, Run' are not much of an exaggeration for these athletes, and it can be an exceedingly dull existence. Non-elite athletes aren't completely immune, either. It's amazingly easy to fall into a bad pattern of exercise addiction, where a growing obsession with working out begins to interfere with work or personal life. This is as much a problem as lack of motivation, because you not only burn out quickly, you also miss out on a lot of fun things in life. And that truly defeats the whole purpose of exercise, which is supposed to enhance these very things.

Small changes in your daily routine can help fend off the depressing, demoralising effects of overtraining, which is why the I.T. programme includes a full week of active rest days every four to eight weeks. Such extended rest periods are an important element of this exercise plan and can save you the embarrassment of falling asleep before the nine o'clock news on TV.

If you do find yourself getting irritable, tired, sore, and apathetic or if workouts are becoming a real struggle, you're definitely pushing yourself too hard. In some respects, this is a milestone to be celebrated. Given the increasingly sedentary nature of our lifestyles these days, most people never even get a glimpse of their own physical capabilities, let alone embrace them. This is why cardiovascular disease is one of the greatest causes of death in this country. You, on the other hand, have successfully managed to truly get out there on the edge.

It's a delicate balance. If the symptoms of overtraining last for more than 10 days or so, do the following.

Take some time off from exercise

Three to five exercise-free days can go far to alleviate overtraining. Depending on how burned out you are, this time will either feel like nirvana attained or an eternity in purgatory. Don't feel guilty about this time off – it's a mental health break as much as a physical one. Use the time to catch up on non-athletic activities, maybe going out for drinks with friends or renting a load of videos. Just don't think about working out.

A week of active rest

Substitute active rest days where you normally have an I.T. or XL workout for a full week. Take it easy and don't push yourself.

Resume exercise at a lower intensity

Get back into the swing of working out by resuming exercise at a lower intensity level or with more frequent rest weeks (no more than one every fourth week). Following these steps will help get you back on track after a bout of overtraining and help you to look forward to a good, hard, sweaty workout again. Use the experience to better recognise the onset of overtraining in the future, so you can take steps early to avoid problems and keep moving toward your fitness goals.

If considerable fatigue persists, go back and repeat the rest and recovery formula above. If fatigue still persists after several weeks of rest and reduced training, it's a good idea to see a physician to rule out the possibility of an underlying illness.

Loss of interest

Loss of interest is experienced by many athletes. Unless you thrive on zenlike repetition, doing the same old exercise routine all the time eventually gets to be, well, routine. If you feel good physically but find yourself sleepwalking with boredom through workouts, you obviously need to jazz things up to stay motivated. Here's how using the I.T. programme can help:

I.T. workouts go more quickly

Interval training workouts seem to pass by more quickly. The varied effort level required for interval training relieves the monotony common to purely aerobic workouts.

I.T. workouts offer variety

Each I.T. workout can be structured in various ways so you are always doing something new and interesting. Within a single training week, you might do a workout with longer but fewer repetitions (e.g. five hard reps lasting two minutes) or do more reps for a shorter time (e.g. 15 reps that last 30 seconds). This not only breaks up routine, it also lets you emphasise the aerobic system one time, the anaerobic system the next.

XL workouts build a solid aerobic base

XL workouts build up endurance and a solid aerobic base and also provide a break from the more intense I.T. sessions.

The I.T. programme gets results

There are few things more motivating than seeing and feeling the fruit of your considerable labours. The I.T. programme gets results. You'll see improvement in the quality and quantity of individual workouts, be it in performing more high-intensity repetitions with less effort or in having more than enough endurance to go for an especially challenging XL workout.

And there are still other ways to help keep up your interest.

Make your workouts a habit

Successful exercisers make workouts a habit. Try to exercise at the same time of day and under similar conditions as often as possible. Think of your workouts as scheduled appointments and stick to them. Motivation is a psychological issue as much as it is a physical one, and if you train your mind and body to anticipate exercise at a certain time and place each day, it becomes almost second nature. You are not only prepared to work, you look forward to it and may even feel slightly out of sorts when you can't squeeze in a workout. It's a chance to devote time solely to yourself, away from the pressures of career, kids, e-mail and phones. As noted before, however, be careful not to allow your habit to become too rigid. You might find yourself in a psychological slump if something prevents you from sticking to your workout schedule. This is a common experience for many athletes who suffer an injury and have to take a lengthy break from exercise.

Cross train

Cross training with other sports and physical activities does wonders to break up the monotony of repetitive exercise, and it aids overall conditioning by calling into use different muscles and movements. (See Chapter 7 for tips on incorporating cross training into your programme.)

Exercise with others

Exercising with a friend or a group of others, even on a sporadic basis, can be a fun and sociable thing to do. The mere fact that you have a standing commitment to show up – which is half the battle on days when you're in a slump and have no interest in working out – is reason enough to enlist the support of others. There's something about being surrounded by like-minded individuals that truly hones the motivational edge. They can provide encouragement and even an added spark of friendly competition, both of which can help push you to perform better than ever.

There are a few things to keep in mind, however. Limit your sessions with others to no more than three times a week, perhaps only on days scheduled for harder workouts. This allows you to recover more fully between hard exercise sessions, because you're free to do your active rest workouts at your own easy pace. Another thing to remember is that exercising with someone else doesn't mean you have to compete with each other or even do the same workout. Focus on doing what's right for you and coordinate things so that you and your friend finish about the same time. It's rare for two individuals to be at identical fitness levels, so don't worry if you do a little more or less than whoever you work out with. When we do I.T. workouts at the track with friends, whoever is less fit runs half or two-thirds of each repetition with the stronger runner, then takes a bit longer rest interval as the other completes the full repetition. It works for us.

Listen to music – or don't!

Listening to music is a crucial tool for some people to maintain motivation when exercising. At big competitions, many athletes can be found off in a corner somewhere with a set of headphones, either psyching themselves up or trying to relax before their event with their favourite tunes. Music can make time pass more enjoyably, especially during some of those seemingly endless XL workouts, and can make getting through those last few I.T. repetitions a little easier, too. You could make your own tapes or CDs to play during workouts, to use for a prerace energy boost, or to wind down after a particularly gruelling session. But it's a matter of individual taste. There are an equal number of purists out there who like things to be quiet when they work out and find that music distracts them from the feedback provided by their own bodies. One of the authors of this book is squarely in this latter camp; the other is just as stubborn about the advantages of the former. Do whatever works for you! Those music lovers who exercise out of doors wearing personal stereos need to be extra-vigilant of vehicle and pedestrian traffic, and women should also be very aware of their surroundings. If you find yourself getting into unfamiliar territory, switch off the music and keep your ears open to what's going on around you instead. Personal safety is the most important thing.

Keep a training log

We swear by keeping a training log and so do countless other athletes. Since many of us can't recall what we had for breakfast, let alone what we did for a workout weeks ago, a training log is invaluable to chart how far you've come, and what works and what doesn't work. Flipping through an old training log can be a truly satisfying experience, as it tells you just how much you've accomplished over time. Set aside a special notebook or make daily notations on a calendar to record what you did for your workout, as well as how you felt that day – several days of 'feel great' sessions obviously indicate that training is optimal, while multiple 'low' entries (when you're tired, sluggish, or apathetic) point towards possible overtraining. Being able to see this at a glance can help nip problems in the bud—before they turn into chronic issues. Some people also record their diet or their resting pulse rate, taken a few minutes after waking up in the morning (a continuously elevated resting heart rate can indicate overtraining, a good sign to back off a bit on workouts). There's a sample training log at the back of this book that can be photocopied and used to track your own progress, and there are several versions you can buy at bookstores or sporting goods shops. A simple notebook with hand-drawn columns works just as well.

Put on your shoes

Sometimes the hardest part of working out can be just overcoming inertia. On days when you have absolutely no interest in working out, focus on putting on your shoes, your swimming costume or loading the bike into the car – the battle's half won right there. Then tell yourself to do only the first five minutes of your workout. Usually, once you start moving, you're likely to continue – it works for us. If you still feel awful after five minutes, stop the workout and take a day off.

Problems with goal setting

Working toward a goal is psychologically easier than working without one. But since many of us haven't got a clue about what we are truly capable of, setting an appropriate goal can present a bit of a problem – or two problems, as it usually turns out.

Overly high expectations

Some people are so excited about the prospect of a new workout programme that they succumb to delusions of grandeur. It's admirable to think big, but we're all limited by genetics and by our many day to day responsibilities, so beware of overly high expectations. To be perfectly honest, many elite athletes are genetic freaks (in the best possible sense, of course) and have natural abilities that the rest of us just plain don't have – and never will. Most of us aren't able to train for under four minute miles while juggling a full-time career or medical school (as Dr Roger Bannister somehow managed to do). Attempting to do so will only result in overtraining, discouragement, frustration, or injury.

Non-existent expectations

The antithesis of the behaviour described above is to carry on without any expectations whatsoever. A lacklustre approach to exercise, such as vaguely vowing to get into shape, can be just as counterproductive as setting overly ambitious goals. What will motivate you to put your shoes on when it's pouring rain outside? When there's a pizza in the freezer? When your favourite programme is on TV?

It might help to think of each workout as a deposit into a savings account. It's easier to make deposits when you are saving up for something specific –

like a trip to the sun or a new car – isn't it? Some athletes begin training for a specific race up to nine months in advance. These folks obviously aren't pushing themselves with undefined goals. They know exactly what they want and carefully plan every step it's going to take for them to get there. That's strong goal orientation, and it can do wonders for your motivation, too.

Realistic goal setting, done with both feet planted squarely on the ground, can be the best motivational tool around. Here are a few guidelines to help you create some attainable goals.

Think of the big picture
Start out by considering the big picture – why are you exercising? Is it to increase fitness, to lose weight or to increase your overall sense of well being? Use this fundamental reason to provide a framework for your I.T. programme.

Think specifics
Once you establish exactly why you're working out, think specifics and set your sights on a clear goal. It may be an athletic goal (such as finishing a 10 km race or hiking to the top of a nearby mountain) or it may be more aesthetically oriented (fitting into your old jeans again). Then find something to visually remind you of the goal, put it where you can see it every day and get to work.

Be realistic!
As with New Year's resolutions, it can be self-defeating to be overly ambitious. Be realistic and set attainable goals that you can feel good about achieving.

Small steps work best
It works best to break your goal into achievable steps (or 'easily digestible chunks', as a friend of ours likes to put it). Jog a mile, then two, then three, before tackling a 5 km race. Hopefully, once you accomplish a particular goal, you'll be pumped up enough to set a new, more ambitious goal. Perhaps a 10 km race? But first …

Reward yourself
Ah, the best part. Reward yourself. Savour the moment before rushing off on yet another quest. Take a deep breath and tell yourself how wonderful you are, enjoy a well-deserved drink after a race with your friends, buy a slinky dress after dropping those last few kilos. Maybe even treat yourself to a holiday. Joseph went to Hawaii after qualifying for the Olympic Trials with a marathon time of 2 hours 18 minutes (and basically just waddled from the pool to the buffet table and back for a week). Rest and recover! Bask in your achievement for a while, then move on to the next goal on your list.

Beyond I.T. — diet, strength training, cross training, stretching and injury prevention

The I.T. programme is an efficient, scientifically and clinically proven method of increasing fitness, burning calories, building more lean muscle mass, and greatly improving your cardiovascular system function. As a stand-alone programme it definitely produces results.

But is the I.T. programme enough?

You can make the results even more dramatic by incorporating into it better nutrition, strength training, cross training, stretching and injury prevention measures. Whole books have been written about each of these topics by experts in their particular fields (which, in these areas at least, we readily admit we are not). But for the purpose of this book, some comments on these subjects from an athlete's perspective and an overview of how each can accentuate the I.T. programme may be of interest to you.

Diet

People love to talk about their latest diet. The Zone Diet, the Pritikin Diet, the Grapefruit Diet, the Cabbage Soup Diet (we're not making this up) are just a few. There's usually a gimmick of some sort involved: counting points, measuring food portions, eating certain food combinations, eating only at certain times of day. And, the people who dream up these gimmicks are, of course, making a fortune.

Perhaps you've experienced some success yourself with a fad diet at one time or another. Why is this?

It's because any diet has the potential to work, initially, simply because followers are thinking about what they put into their mouths.

People who are conscious of their eating habits tend to eat less. But any diet that withholds adequate calories and nutrients or eliminates whole food groups or is too cumbersome to keep up on a long-term basis is doomed to failure. Millions of overweight people all too often discover this for themselves.

The high-intensity nature of the I.T. programme calls for some special nutritional considerations, and you might actually need to eat more calories, not less, to maintain a healthy weight. Your body needs fuel for peak performance. Dramatic changes to your diet probably aren't necessary – just a tweak here and there can really make a difference. If you think your eating habits could use a more extensive overhaul, consult a nutritionist or doctor. Here are a few more things to keep in mind.

A calorie is a calorie

A calorie is a calorie. The body makes no distinction between 500 calories worth of chocolate cake and 500 calories of carrot sticks; all it sees is 500 units of stored energy. The body uses whatever happens to be lying around. This isn't to say that a 100 per cent protein diet or a 100 per cent carbohydrate diet or a 100 per cent fat diet would all affect the body the same way. Each of these energy sources has its place: protein is needed to build muscle and other tissues; carbohydrates are a main fuel source for the brain and working muscles; fat serves as an efficient source of calories to all systems. This is why experts always harp on the need to have a well-balanced diet with a variety of foods from all three sources.

There's no secret to long-term weight loss

To lose weight you need to burn more calories than you take in. That's it. **The only natural ways to create this calorie deficit are to eat less, exercise more or do a combination of both.** Studies show that people doing the combined plan lose weight faster and are more successful at keeping it off – so **eat sensibly and exercise regularly**.

Calories are fuel for your body

You won't find many elite athletes on wacky, ultra-restrictive diets. They treat their bodies like machines, fuelling them well to keep things operating at peak levels. Eat when you're genuinely hungry, because that's a signal that you're running low on energy. For the first few weeks of the I.T. programme, you may be hungrier than usual, but it'll level out soon enough. Does all that hard exercise give you free rein to stuff your face with junk food or eat double portions? No. Instead, add a bit more to your regular meals or have nutritious mini meals, perhaps every three or four hours, and stop eating when you aren't hungry anymore. It seems ridiculously easy, but it may take time to adjust to this sort of natural eating.

Athletes need carbohydrates

Skimping on daily carbohydrate intake can actually hinder your I.T. programme. Athletes need them. You burn carbohydrate and some fat during aerobic workouts, but for harder, anaerobic sessions the primary fuel comes from carbohydrates. And, since the body's limited glycogen (carbohydrate) stores become depleted very quickly, it's crucial to eat enough carbohydrates when you start doing speedwork. Without them, you'll eventually falter and not have enough energy left in you to push on to the finish line. The same effect can also occur over a period of days or weeks, as glycogen stores are used up faster than they're replaced. So eat carbohydrates, just don't go overboard with them – too many carbohydrates can cause blood sugar levels to swing.

Keep it simple
Complicated, rigid diet plans are a waste of time. To improve eating habits, keep it simple – isolate one unhealthy habit at a time and make changes there. Instead of a tub of ice cream for dessert every night, say, have it once a week, or switch to frozen yogurt. Or vow to quit eating on autopilot, mindlessly plowing through bags of crisps or biscuits in front of the TV. Add more fruit, vegetables and grains so that your daily diet is about 60 per cent carbohydrate, 15 per cent protein, and 25 per cent fat. Focus on doing consistent, high-quality I.T. workouts and forget about obsessively counting calories.

How does metabolism work?
The body's basic unit of energy is the much-maligned calorie (a kilocalorie, technically, but hardly anyone calls it that). Each gram of carbohydrate provides four calories; each gram of protein four calories; and each gram of fat provides nine calories. To gain ½ kilo you need to eat 3500 more calories than your body uses, and to lose a pound you have to burn those same 3500 calories off. No wonder losing weight is so difficult!

What a lot of people don't know is that each gram of stored carbohydrate retains nine grams of water, while protein and fat store little or no water. This is why those popular high protein/low carb diets produce such amazing results in the first few weeks. Basically, when few carbohydrates are eaten, the body turns to stored carbohydrates for energy and that retained water is released and flushed out of the system. The weight lost isn't fat – it's mostly water weight. While preparing for a marathon, Joseph avoided carbohydrates for three days to deplete glycogen stores as part of a carbohydrate-loading regime. In that brief time, his weight dropped from 154 to 147 pounds, despite training only half as much as usual. But then, after three days of eating carbs again, he was back at his usual weight again. Did he somehow manage to lose and then regain almost 25,000 calories in six days? Of course not. It was all water weight.

Eating too much protein can cause irritability and fatigue because the brain – which feeds primarily on carbohydrates – isn't getting the calories it needs to maintain its everyday functions. High-protein diets are tough on the kidneys and make for rather limited dining options too, so it's probably for the best that most people can't stick to this sort of eating for very long. Of course, some protein is necessary, especially for people who do higher intensity exercise. A little common sense and moderation go a long way.

Is it possible to manipulate metabolism with fad diets? Sure, but only briefly. The body eventually fights off any self-imposed starvation by going into an energy-saving mode, making you too sluggish to squander precious calories exercising. It's a natural survival mechanism, and judging by the number of glassy-eyed couch potatoes out there, it works really, really well. Crafty schemes to drop weight fast tend to backfire with the dreaded yo-yo effect: the metabolism drops until the body eventually revolts and demands food in an effort to shore up against any future 'famines'. The net result is weight gain. So just use your common sense – it's not clever to mess with Mother Nature.

What should I eat before, during and after an I.T. or XL workout?

Eating pre-workout

Hard exercise temporarily slows down your digestion, which explains why your sandwich sits in your stomach like a rock when you go running straight after lunch. But doing a workout on a completely empty stomach isn't too clever either, as it can leave you hypoglycaemic and unmotivated. Many athletes find that exercising when they're slightly hungry seems to work best – there's not a heavy meal in the stomach, and the physical exertion usually releases enough glucose and fat into the bloodstream to make it through the session. If you must eat, and plan to train in less than an hour, a sports drink packing easy-to-digest carbohydrate might do the trick. If you want something more, make sure it's light and mostly carbohydrate, so you won't be running on empty but can still exercise comfortably. (A piece of toast with a thin spread of peanut butter, a sports drink or half a banana should do it.) Some people who exercise first thing in the morning find that having a midnight snack carries them through their workout nicely. Try to avoid fatty foods before a workout – they're a chore to digest and leave you feeling sluggish. Energy bars? There are many out there to pick and choose from, but to be honest, many elite athletes never eat them. They pack up to 300 calories and more protein than you need in an entire day and don't do anything magical for your body or your performance, either. Some taste terrible and others are really just confectionary bars in disguise. But if you like them, they're fine for a pre-workout snack.

Eating during a workout

You won't want to eat anything during an I.T. workout, but it's a different story with the longer XL sessions. There's nothing worse than being at the turnaround point of a 40 mile bike ride and feeling too dehydrated or hypoglycaemic to get all the way back home. Make sure you take along a bottle of water, diluted fruit juice or a sports drink (250 ml for every 20 minutes of exercise) and a small, easily absorbed snack such as raisins or a banana. Research shows that simple carbohydrates eaten during a long bout of exercise are used as a source of energy by working muscles, preserving the glycogen (carbohydrate) stores. If you're setting off for a really long endurance workout, particularly if it's a warm day, bring a light, high-carbohydrate, salty snack (such as pretzels or crisps) to replace sodium lost in sweat.

Do I need to take vitamins or supplements?

Taking a simple multivitamin is useful for anyone whose diet isn't as balanced as it could be, as well as for teenagers, vegetarians, vegans and pregnant women. Nutrients should ideally come only from whole foods, but you may find that it's just more practical to take vitamins to fill in nutritional gaps. More isn't necessarily better when it comes to vitamins, so take the recommended dosage and leave it at that. Another thing: vitamins are vitamins, so opt for the cheaper generic versions over expensive name brands. It's all the same on the inside, just slicker packaging and marketing on the outside.

Eating post-workout
Remember to refuel. Research shows that having a simple high carbohydrate snack either immediately after or two hours after an intense workout is the best way to replace depleted glycogen stores. Rehydrating is important too, and few things quench thirst better than plain old water. Later on, you'll probably be ravenous and ready to tear the door off the refrigerator. Have something with enough calories to replace whatever you burned off. Many athletes stick to high carbohydrate staples such as pasta, rice, potatoes and bread for their post-workout meals. These are fine, but add some fat so you won't be hungry again for a while. Toss in some fruit and vegetables too; they contain antioxidants that help fend off muscle damage and injury.

Hydration do's and don't's
Coaches and trainers all over the world make the same complaint about their elite athletes: they're chronically dehydrated. You probably are too. The body is 50 to 65 per cent water and needs to be constantly topped up. Exercising hard increases fluid loss since water is excreted as sweat to cool things down. Dehydration causes the blood to thicken and forces the heart to work harder. It slows the delivery of oxygen and nutrients to the muscles and can leave you sluggish and unable to concentrate. It also lowers your ability to tolerate lactic acid, which makes you feel exhausted faster. It's basically bad all round, so drink up! If possible, take in at least four to eight ounces of fluid every 15 to 20 minutes when exercising hard, and more if it's a hot day. Don't wait until you're thirsty – that's a sign you're already dehydrated. Good rules of thumb: drink twice as much as it takes to quench your thirst; drink enough that your urine is clear or light yellow in color; keep caffeinated drinks and alcohol to a minimum (they're dehydrating); and follow every workout with at least *24 ounces* of water or a sports drink. Which sports drink is best? Here's a quick rundown.

Regular sports drinks
Sports drinks are great to swig down before or during a workout and may even be a better option than water during long, hot endurance sessions. All sports drinks include electrolytes such as sodium and potassium, which are important whenever you sweat heavily.

Fitness water
Tastier than plain water, fitness waters are flavoured drinks with 10 to 25 calories per 250 ml bottle, a touch of sodium and potassium, and even a few vitamins, perfect for workouts lasting less than an hour when you don't need the high calories of a sports drink. Watered-down fruit juice works well too.

Recovery drinks
High-calorie recovery drinks are ideal for before or after exercise when a good boost of carbohydrates (about 160 to 240 calories per 250 ml bottle) comes in handy. Use them in place of solid food before a hard workout or as a snack afterward to tide you over until a meal time.

Strength training
Strength training is an important part of the I.T. programme. Any workout programme that focuses primarily on cardiovascular development can leave certain muscle groups more or less neglected. You've probably seen how distance runners have well-developed leg muscles with comparatively scrawny upper bodies, with swimmers just the reverse. To some degree, this can actually offer some competitive advantage. In the gruelling Tour de France, for example, heavily muscled legs are necessary, but a heavily muscled upper body only serves as extra weight to haul up steep mountain climbs. When Lance Armstrong returned to the Tour having lost weight after a long bout of chemotherapy, his leaner upper body was a factor that helped propel him to the winner's podium.

For those of you who aren't training for the Tour (yet), it's a good idea to add strength training to your I.T. programme to strike a balance between the primarily used 'I.T. muscles' and the rest of the body. Strength training offers several advantages.

Injury prevention
Maintaining a balance between opposing muscle groups can prevent injury by protecting against a 'weak link' failure.

Muscle adaptation
Much like an I.T. workout, intense strength work (that is, working to muscle failure) causes muscle adaptation, a higher metabolic rate, and greater strength.

A complete package
A full-body strengthening regime develops a more complete package by increasing overall body fitness, improving the physique, and boosting self-image.

Strength training offers benefits extending beyond mere fitness, such as building up bone mass to stave off osteoporosis in women. All that's needed are a few pieces of equipment and a handful of extra minutes a week. You can give yourself an in-depth crash course on strength training by consulting any one of the many books and magazines currently out there on the subject. For now, here are a few thoughts to get you started:

Strength training should supplement the I.T. programme

If your time is too limited to handle both strength training and the I.T. programme, focus energy on the latter. However, recent studies suggest that nearly as much benefit can be had from a single set of weight repetitions as from multiple sets, so it may be possible to squeeze in some training after all. You won't end up looking like Arnold Schwarzenegger doing this sort of abbreviated weight routine, but at a pinch, one set might do the trick.

Strength train two to three days a week

Most people do strength work on active rest days, two to three days a week, when their shorter workout allows extra time to lift weights. Any time is fine; the goal is merely to get it done. Allow at least a full day between sessions to give muscles a chance to recover and rebuild.

Focus on neglected muscle groups

Don't overburden yourself with dozens of exercises. Instead, focus on neglected muscle groups. Otherwise, you'll just spend more time in the gym, cutting in on time better devoted to cardiovascular training. A handful of well-selected exercises that can be done quickly and consistently will suffice.

Do minimal strength training for I.T. muscles

Many athletes think strengthening their primary movers (the main muscles used for a given activity, such as calf muscles for running) provides added power and speed. There may be some merit to this, but usually these muscles are already working hard just doing the I.T. programme and need minimal additional strengthening. At least for the first few months of more intense workouts, concentrate only on more neglected muscle groups, such as upper body muscles for walkers, runners, cyclists and people who use stair climbers and similar machines.

Keep a written log

Keep track of your strength training with a written log, just as you do for your other I.T. programme workouts. Include the number of sets, number of reps, and amount of weight lifted for each exercise. At the very least, the log will remind you where to set the weight next time you lift; even better, it will show you how much stronger you are getting. Nothing beats tangible evidence of improvement for motivation.

Do alternative exercises

They're just what they say they are – alternative exercises to your regular strength-training regime. Leave the dumbbells in the closet and use your own body weight or something else instead. Do slow push-ups with good form to isolate the chest, shoulders and triceps. Use family-sized cans of beans or buckets or plastic jugs filled with water or sand – anything that weighs a couple of kilos. Take advantage of the workout stations found in some public parks or recreation areas. Do tricep dips on a chair or bench, climb a rope, play with rubber resistance bands, or bench-press the dog! The idea is to add some variety and fun to what can sometimes be rather dull work. Some suggestions are listed below.

Mix it up

Add variety by mixing things up a bit. You can do your strength-training exercises as straight sets (doing one to three sets of each exercise before moving on to the next), as circuits (doing one set of several different exercises, then repeating), or as supersets (doing 1 set each of two consecutive exercises, such as chest/back or biceps/triceps and then resting).

With the exception of swimming, most activities involved with the I.T. programme focus on leg muscles, so your strength training should emphasize upper body and trunk work. Here's a sample workout week for someone who has basic strength-training experience. If you're just starting out, choose lighter weights than you think you can handle and do just one set of each exercise. Slowly adjust the weight over the course of a few sessions until you reach muscle failure – when you can't lift the weight anymore. This is your baseline – it's what you're able to lift at your weakest and puniest! From now on, you're only going to get stronger.

Day 1:	1–3 sets of 10–12 repetitions of strength exercises (up to 15 if advanced)
Endurance:	1–3 sets of 10–25 sit-ups and dead lifts
Day 3:	2–3 sets of 3–6 repetitions of strength exercises with slightly heavier weights
Power:	weight (the first set should be a warm-up set with lighter weights)
	1–3 sets of 10–25 sit-ups and dead lifts
Day 5:	alternative exercises

Suggested strength exercises for a fast but thorough upper body workout are described and pictured on the following pages.

Barbell or dumbbell bench press

Lie face up on a flat bench holding a barbell or two dumbbells over the middle of your chest at arm's length, palms facing forwards. Lower the weights until they are just outside your shoulders. Return to the starting position and repeat. Muscles emphasised are the pectoralis major, anterior deltoids, and triceps.

Alternative exercise – push-up

Place your hands on the floor about shoulder width apart, elbows straight but not locked. Slowly lower the chest to the floor, keeping the trunk as stable as possible throughout. Push back up to the starting position and repeat.

Lat pull-down

Sit with your knees supported by the thigh pad, feet flat on floor. Hold the bar with your hands slightly wider than shoulder width apart, palms facing forwards. Keep your abs tight and lean back slightly at the hip as you pull the bar toward your chest. Pause and slowly allow your arms to return to their fully extended position. Repeat. (Avoid doing behind-the-head pull-downs, as they can cause injury.) Muscles emphasised are the latissimus dorsi, trapezius and rhomboids.

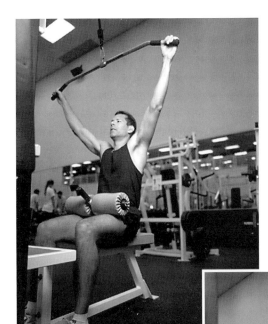

Alternative exercise – chin-up

Hang fully extended from the bar with your hands slightly wider than shoulder width apart, palms facing forwards. Smoothly pull up as far as you can go. Lower your body back down, maintaining full control. Muscles emphasised are the latissimus dorsi, trapezius and rhomboid muscles.

Military press

Hold a barbell across your collarbone with palms facing forwards, hands slightly wider than shoulder width apart. Your elbows should form 90 degree angles directly under the bar. Press the barbell up over your head until your arms are fully extended. Return to the starting position and repeat. Muscles emphasised are the middle deltoids and triceps.

Deadlift

Bend into a squat, feet shoulder width apart, and grasp a barbell with an overhand grip, hands slightly wider than shoulder width apart. Keep your back slightly arched, your chest out, and your eyes looking forward. Slowly stand upright, keeping your arms straight and the bar close to your body. Return to the starting position and repeat. Muscles emphasised are the supraspinatus and infraspinatus.

Alternative exercise – superman

Lie on your stomach with your arms and legs extended. Raise your arms and legs slightly off the ground, hold for a count of five, then lower. Repeat, trying to get your arms and legs a bit higher off the ground each time. Muscles emphasised are the supraspinatus, infraspinatus and erector spinae.

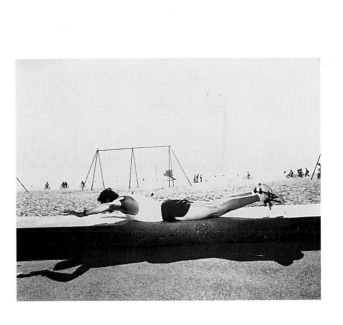

Sit-up

Lie on floor with bent knees, feet flat on the floor, hands unclasped behind your head. Tighten the abdominals and exhale as you slowly curl up, your back neutral, just raising the shoulder blades and upper back toward the pelvis. Hold, then slowly lower and repeat. Work other abdominal muscles by curling up and rotating your left elbow towards your right knee, then right elbow to left knee, and repeat. Muscles emphasised are the rectus abdominus and external and internal obliques.

Leg lift

Using an elevated Roman chair or pull-up bar, support yourself on your forearms with your legs dangling. Lift your knees together so that your thighs are parallel to the floor, then slowly return to the starting position and repeat. Muscles emphasised are the rectus abdominus and the external and internal obliques.

Biceps curl

Hold a barbell or a pair of dumbbells at arm's length, palms turned so that your wrists face forwards. Bend your elbows to raise the weights to your shoulders without moving your upper arms. Return to the starting position and repeat. Muscles emphasised are the biceps.

Alternative exercise – triceps dip

Work the antagonist to the bicep by sitting on a chair or bench, hands gripping the front edge, legs straight out in front of you or slightly bent. Move your hips forward until they're just off the seat, then lower them slowly towards the floor. Press back up until your arms are almost fully extended, but don't lock your elbows. Muscles emphasised are the triceps.

Cross training

Many people feel comfortable doing only 'their thing', be it pounding out miles on the road, swimming lengths, or conquering Everest via the stair climber. Other people go crazy without variety in their workouts and ping-pong from one activity to the next. They're the ones with the garages full of athletic equipment.

There is a third group of people who are prevented by injuries, environment or time constraints from pursuing a particular activity as often as they'd like. Or, maybe they just have a low threshold for boredom and need more variety. This group can have the best of both worlds by cross training or by varying exercise activities. The I.T. programme is well suited to cross training, whether it be an occasional dabble in other waters or a completely integrated multisport workout plan. In fact, there are good reasons why everyone should add a little cross training to their I.T. programme.

Cross training develops different muscles

Cross training with an exercise that is nothing like your usual activity – such as swimming for a stair climbing fanatic or cyclist – develops different, underused muscles and allows more balanced development. Any high intensity exercise improves the cardiovascular system, so there's no fitness advantage to always sticking to a single activity.

Cross training reduces the risk of overuse injuries

For athletes, repetitive motion can cause overuse injuries, such as stress fractures in runners' feet or saddle sores for cyclists. Cross training with alternative activities, even if only once in a blue moon, can help reduce the risk of overuse injuries. It can also prevent burnout, another symptom of overtraining, usually characterised by lingering aches and pains, troubled sleep, loss of appetite, weight loss, persistent colds, listlessness, sluggishness and irritability.

Cross training can be more interesting

No doubt about it, a change now and then can be psychologically stimulating. Cross training adds interest and keeps you out of workout ruts.

Here's how to best incorporate cross training into your I.T. programme. Try one new activity once or twice a week on active rest days, doing roughly two-thirds of your baseline workout. Don't do any hard workouts with this new activity until your body gets used to the new demands. Active rest days are meant for recovery, so save your energy for the more intense I.T. and XL workouts.

If you eventually want to take on a different activity for your I.T. and XL workouts every once in a while, there's only one rule: do it hard enough so that you're tired!

This may be tricky at first, when you don't have a well-developed frame of reference and aren't sure how hard to push. If running on a treadmill is your primary I.T. workout, for example, you know what you're capable of in terms of number of repetitions, intensity levels and length of intervals. But in terms of mountain biking, say, your sense of your capabilities may be fuzzier. Can you really make it to the next ridge without running out of steam? It's going to take some experimenting, so just concentrate on getting in a good workout. Try doing it free-form at first: do a short warm-up, then go hard for a bit, then back off, repeating for however long you wish. Or, do it the more traditional way, going one minute at a higher intensity, followed by two minutes of active recovery. Either way, just go for it. Charge the hill! Sprint the next lap! Boldly go to levels you've never gone to before.

If you decide to cross train on a day scheduled for a XL workout, plan on doing it for less time and at an even lower intensity than you would your usual activity. If you want to continue with the new activity, slowly adjust variables over the course of several sessions until you reach an optimal I.T. and XL workout. Keep an open mind, too – you may find you like the new cross-training activity better, and eventually switch so that it's your primary form of exercise. Continue to strike a balance between the different types of I.T. workouts, doing longer repetitions some days and shorter ones the next, varying the number of reps, intensity level and interval length, emphasising both aerobic and anaerobic systems. Of course, if you don't want to push yourself hard with this new activity, just do it for fun and to break the monotony on active rest days.

Stretching

It's hard to believe how much debate there has been over the years about such a simple thing as stretching. Experts argue over when it should be done, how much it should be done and even whether it should be done at all. All things considered, stretching – if done correctly – can be highly beneficial. And yet there are many of us who still think of stretching as we think of flossing – a necessary evil, something that's good for us but has to be endured. Many athletes skip the stretching portion of their workout entirely, opting instead to cram in an extra repetition or two. But a better plan would be skip those last few reps and devote some quality minutes to improving flexibility instead.

It's a proven fact that the range of motion of joints decreases with age, as muscles, tendons and ligaments grow stiffer and lose elasticity. This, coupled with the fact that muscles tend to tighten and shorten with greater use, means that loss of flexibility is inevitable unless you put up a determined fight against it. Many athletes learn this the hard way. There are any number of runners out there, for example, who find it impossible to touch their toes! You can spot them at the side of the track, hunched in vain over their stiff-as-a-board hamstrings.

Why is flexibility such a big deal? For one thing, good flexibility is a factor in staying injury-free. No one really can say just why this is, but there seems to be a connection between lack of flexibility and exercise-induced muscle damage (micro tears, not acute strains or sprains). A regular programme of stretching not only helps restore lost flexibility, but it also helps prevent further losses, reduces post-exercise soreness and soothes stressed-out minds. Exercise just feels better when the body is supple and well stretched out. Tight neck and shoulder muscles, for example, can affect form just as much as tight hamstrings. In short, stretching is time well spent. Here are a few tips for making it part of your daily routine.

Don't stretch cold muscles and joints

It's enough to make us cringe sometimes, remembering how people once advised thorough stretching before warming up. Yikes. Stretching cold muscles and joints is one sure way to do serious damage. You can avoid this by warming up a bit first, doing a few minutes of light exercise, doing your stretches and **then** starting the more intense part of your workout. Or, stretch afterwards, as many people seem to prefer. Sometimes, the best part of a hard workout is the leisurely stretch that follows it.

Stretch gently

Stretch often, and stretch gently. Too many exercisers just grab a leg and yank it back for a second or two or, even worse, stretch by bouncing. Other people stretch too long – a stretch really shouldn't be held more than 30 seconds or so. Scary fact: once a connective tissue (a ligament or tendon) is over-stretched, it never returns to its normal length, and the joint associated with it will always be less stable. Don't try to pull yourself into dramatically deeper stretches. These simply activate the stretch reflex, causing the muscle to contract as self-protection against possible injury. Keep it gentle, brief and as smooth and steady as possible.

Stretching shouldn't be painful

You should feel tension when you stretch – if it hurts, you're overdoing it and should back off, immediately. Slowly exhale and lean into the stretch just until you feel mild discomfort, then ease off a bit and hold for about 30 seconds.

Good form is key

It's absurdly easy to be lazy and cheat when stretching, which can cause more harm than doing no stretching at all. Maintain good form by keeping the number of stretches you do down to a minimum, so you can really concentrate on what you're doing.

Do one minute of stretching for every 10 minutes of exercise

Some athletes figure that two minutes of fast, sloppy stretches after a workout means they've stretched. It doesn't. A good rule of thumb is to do one minute of stretching for every 10 minutes of exercise. Allow enough time after each and every workout for a full body session, working – at the very least – the calves, hamstrings, quadriceps, lower back, shoulders and neck.

Be patient

Improving flexibility is no different from trying to get stronger or faster; it takes time and practice. Be patient and do it consistently and you'll see improvements in your range of motion.

Quadriceps stretch

Hold your ankle in one hand and gently pull your heel towards your rear end. Hold onto a wall or chair if necessary to maintain balance. Flex the foot to increase the stretch along the front of the thigh. Don't let your bent leg drift out to the side, which puts stress on the knee. Keep your hips tucked under, your back straight and try not to lean forward.

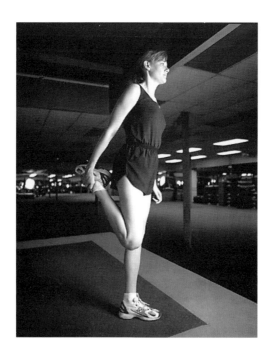

Hamstring stretch

Prop up your leg at knee height (not hip height) or even lower to reduce the risk of injury. Bend your knee slightly and gently lean forward, keeping your back straight. You can also lie on your back, with one leg bent with the foot on the floor and the other leg upright. Pull the upright leg towards your chest with the knee slightly bent.

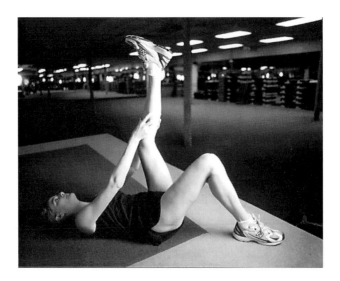

Hip flexor stretch

Lunge forward with your right foot, knee bent at a 90 degree angle directly over the ankle, left leg extended behind you. Lean your chest forward and let your hips sink toward the floor. Another good move: lie on your back, knees bent, feet flat on the floor. Cross the left ankle in front of the right knee. Clasp your hands behind the right knee and gently pull it towards your chest, using it as a lever to stretch the left hip. Be careful to keep the right leg bent and hold for about 30 seconds.

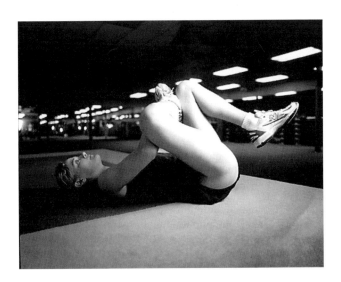

Calf stretch

The popular way to do this stretch is to hang the heels off a step, which can tear muscles and tendons. A better method is to prop your toes against a wall, step or tree with the heel on the ground. You can also plant both feet on the ground and lean forward, pushing against a wall or other surface.

Neck and shoulder stretch

This is a good stretch to relieve tension and tightness in the neck and shoulders, especially for runners who let their shoulders drift towards their ears at faster paces and cyclists who hunch over their handlebars too long. Sit with a straight back, tip your head towards your chest and hold. You may lightly touch the back of your head to enhance the stretch a bit. Do the same from side to side, gently tilting your ear towards your shoulder. You can also lie on your back, tucking your chin towards your chest while flexing your feet. Hold for a few seconds, then relax and release all tension. Try it in bed at night just before going to sleep.

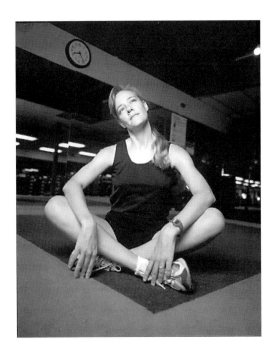

Figure 4 stretch

Sit on the floor with one leg extended in front of you, toes pointed up. Bend the other leg so the sole of the foot rests against the opposite thigh just below your groin (making a '4'). Lean forward, reaching for your toes with both arms and exhale while keeping a straight back until you feel the stretch.

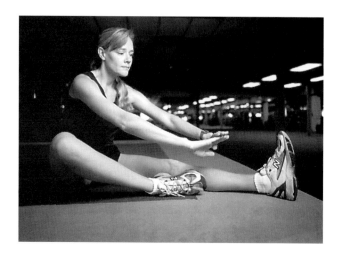

Injury prevention

Athletes and injuries seem to go together, usually because we do too much, too fast, with too little time set aside for rest and recovery. There are many ways to avoid injury, however, and quick action to counter minor problems can keep them from turning into chronic ones.

The single best way to prevent injury is to avoid overtraining. Cross train and strength train to help develop other muscle groups and provide balance and rest for your primary movers. Watch for early signs of burnout. And, learn to recognise differences in pain.

Good pain v harmful pain

'Good pain' is common, exercise-induced muscle soreness and is often relieved by a warm-up. 'Harmful pain' is not relieved by a warm-up or rest and indicates a genuine injury. Some other fine-line distinctions between the two are as follows:

- Muscle soreness is mildly uncomfortable and disappears rapidly. An injury usually feels more acute, like a sharp jolt of electricity or a pop, and lasts longer. (Exceptions are overuse injuries, which tend to have a more gradual onset.)

- Overuse injuries (such as stress fractures) come about from the wear and tear of repetitive movement, such as running and cycling. These injuries may have no obvious cause and often don't seem like a big deal at first – they're just a dull, annoying pain. But these injuries are actually hairline fractures in bone or microtears in muscle and, if ignored, can turn into bigger problems.

- Muscle soreness tends to be on both sides of the body, while injury is usually one-sided.

- Injury tends to be more point specific ('It hurts here'), while muscle soreness is more diffuse.

- Soreness usually goes away after a day or two. It responds well to R.I.C.E. (rest, ice, compression and elevation) and anti-inflammatories, such as ibuprofen. Pain associated with an injury lingers longer.

Tips to avoid injury

When you feel pain, stop immediately

Often you don't feel any pain until the damage is already done, so you'll just make things worse by struggling to work through it.

Slowly increase training intensity over time

Don't fall into the trap of doing too much, too soon. Increase each variable one at a time and listen to your body.

Limit hard training to four to eight week periods

Limit hard training to four to eight week periods, then ease off to give your body a breather. You can't continually increase training intensity without a break – push hard enough, long enough and your body will eventually come to a screeching halt. Maintain control over your workout programme by factoring in recovery periods before your body reaches the breaking point. Elite athletes are no exception.

Use good form and technique

Sacrificing good form and technique in order to finish a tough workout session means you're not fully in control of your body – and that's when injuries happen.

Don't skimp on active rest days

Surprisingly, light exercise can promote healing faster than lying on the sofa all day. So don't skimp on active rest days – get moving!

Try cross training while recovering from injury

Don't use injury as an excuse to become a complete slug (unless it's severe, of course). Instead, try cross training while you recover. Do what's pain free – if you have shin splints, try swimming. Shoulder problems? Get on a bike instead or 'run' in a pool to avoid heavy pounding, as many competitive athletes often do. Cross training will keep you fit and also prevent the muscle imbalances and inflexibility that come from doing only a single sport.

What to do if you're feeling pain? Take a few days off with R.I.C.E., the basic first aid for any sport-related injury.

Rest

Rest, by backing off completely for a few days, or find a light, nonaggravating exercise to do until you fully recover.

Ice

Apply ice, a cold pack, or a bag of frozen peas for 10 to 15 minutes every two to four hours to relieve pain and reduce any swelling. (If the swelling is down after 48 hours of ice treatments, do a little heat treatment to speed up the healing process, using heat pads, moist hot packs or hot baths.)

Compression

Put on an elastic wrap, with firm but comfortable pressure, during and after an ice treatment. Make sure you take it off before sleeping.

Elevation

Prop up the injured area so it's elevated above heart level whenever possible.

You might take some aspirin or ibuprofen to reduce pain and swelling too, but read the dosage information carefully and don't start popping them like candy (as too many athletes tend to do). You shouldn't have to take a pain reliever to get through a workout! And, don't make the mistake of trying to exercise through the pain, especially if there's any chance you have more acute tissue damage. Some world-class athletes do this and seem to bounce right back after injury – but they have experts to diagnose and treat them immediately, they're in tip-top condition, and they're highly motivated to recover. Stop exercising whenever there's pain beyond mild discomfort, and rest to avoid aggravating the problem. If there's no improvement or the pain gets worse, see an orthopaedist, a specialist in musculoskeletal and joint problems.

There's no question that you're going to experience some muscle soreness doing the I.T. programme. The greater intensity leaves most people feeling it for a day or two after a hard workout. But continued soreness should be countered by skipping the next I.T. or XL workout and taking one to three days off. Resume exercise with a few active rest days once you're pain-free again, then go back to I.T. and XL workouts at a slightly lower intensity for a few sessions. Don't worry about losing speed or endurance when taking time off to recover from injury – you won't lose fitness as quickly as you might think. Keep the big picture in mind. An injury is a minor setback when caught early enough, and time on the sofa can keep it from becoming serious enough to really interfere with your workout schedule.

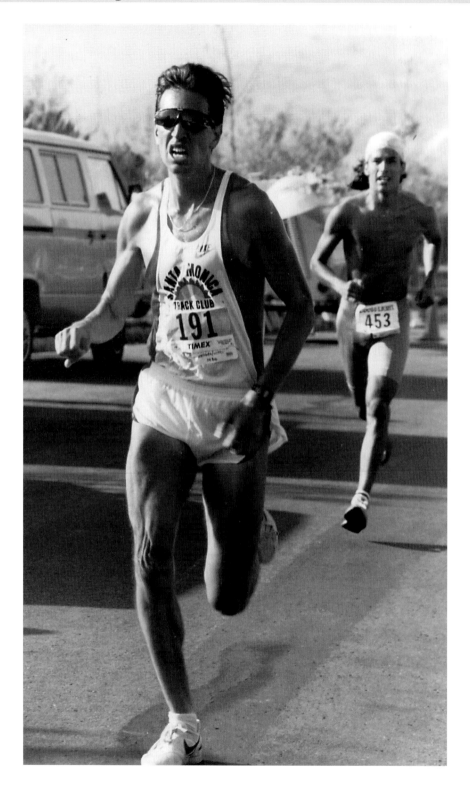

8 The I.T. competitive edge programme

The roar of the crowd is deafening as you surge from the pack on the way to certain victory. The finish line comes into view, your outstretched arms wave to the screaming crowd, and…

You wake up.

Okay, so most of us compete better in our dreams than in reality. But that doesn't mean it's impossible to set personal records and feel the same pride as the ones with gold medals around their necks. The I.T. Programme works because it employs the same basic training methods used by elite athletes, and the principles of physiologic adaptation are the same for everyone from Olympic champions to weekend runners in local races.

The rigours of athletic competition aren't for everyone. Some people want nothing at all to do with it. They exercise strictly for fitness or fun or a sense of well-being, and if they do enter a race, it's to raise money for a good cause or a chance to wear a crazy team costume with the gang from the office. And that's fine. If that's the case you might want to skip the rest of this chapter, which is written for those who think the whole point of exercise is to push their limitations, a chance to get out there and see what they can do. When a good race rolls around, they sign up, do their best and head home wearing a new T-shirt and a smug, satisfied smile. Or – as it often happens – they wonder if they could have done better and how they might improve their results next time.

Performing at peak level requires a master plan, a carefully choreographed mix of workouts designed to get the most out of your body – the I.T. competitive edge programme. This training schedule is even more challenging than the standard I.T. programme and requires discipline and a strong drive to go faster than ever before. Accepting the challenge – and the fatigue and aching muscles that invariably go along with it – can bring you closer to fulfilling your true physical potential than you may have believed possible.

Choose a challenge

First things first: select a specific challenge for yourself, something to genuinely test your capabilities. The key word here is 'specific'. Instead of a wishy-washy vow to 'run faster', say 'I want to run a 5 km in under 17 minutes' or 'I want to cycle from here to Oxford in two hours'. As in so many other aspects of life, having a specific destination is the only way to ever get anywhere.

This challenge can be done as a time trial or as part of an organised competition. A time trial is a full-effort exertion done over a particular distance, such as a one mile swim, and it's just you racing against the clock. Time trials are a good way to track progress, but they have one significant drawback: you cannot replicate the feel of a race in training, no matter how intensely you work out. That's why personal bests – and world records – are rarely (if ever) recorded alone, even by the most talented, motivated athlete. Because of this, we'll stick to discussing organised competitions, such as swimming, running or cycling competitions, in which the adrenaline rush of going head-to-head with other athletes can lead to faster times than you might reach on your own.

Timing is everything

Successful competitors know that timing is everything. Find a race that's at least four months away, preferably six. Attaining peak fitness involves much more than a quick pre-race tune-up – you need enough time to give your training a real overhaul. Elite athletes often train for six months to a year

Pushing the boundaries: the anaerobic threshold

The I.T. programme prepares you for the rigours of competition by increasing the body's anaerobic threshold, or AT. As long as there's enough oxygen in a working muscle, and the muscle is able to use that oxygen, exercise is considered aerobic and can keep going for quite some time. As intensity increases, the body's ability to deliver and utilise oxygen to generate energy is overwhelmed, so energy has to be created anaerobically. Breathing is laboured and the heart rate is up to near maximum at this point. Anaerobic metabolism results in the secretion of lactic acid into the blood, where the liver and heart tap into it as an energy source. Above a certain exercise intensity, more of this waste product is produced than can be processed (or cleared) by the body, and it starts to build up in the blood. This level of exercise is known as the 'anaerobic threshold', where the increased amount of lactic acid limits how long the body can continue exercising at a high intensity. That's what hampers performance during workouts and competition.

The I.T. programme helps battle this barrier by training the body to work at higher intensities for longer periods of time before reaching the anaerobic threshold. Long endurance-type workouts, such as XL workouts, delay anaerobic exercise by creating more muscle capillaries and mitochondria to use oxygen more efficiently. Regular I.T. workouts and AT (anaerobic threshold) workouts also increase the rate of lactate clearance and retrain some larger muscle fibres to make better use of oxygen. The net result of all these physical adaptations is the ability to more effectively manage the hard work of a gruelling workout or athletic competition, both physically and psychologically.

before peaking within a four to six week competitive window of opportunity. Then, after a period of much-needed rest and recovery, they start the process all over again. To succeed, you need that same discipline and dedication to get through the tough times, those dark days when you're tired or the water's freezing or it's pouring with rain and the race seems a million years away. But for anyone with a spark of competitive instinct, this is what training is all about. If it were easy, everyone would be doing it, right?

Take small, progressive steps

Plan to do some practice races or individual time trials as your target competition approaches. It's a great way to stay motivated and gives you a good sense of your physical condition. With each race or time trial, your goal is to gain racing experience and progressively lower your times. These smaller, progressive steps are important; no one, no matter how naturally gifted they are, wakes up one morning, decides to take up running, and manages to qualify for the Olympics by dinnertime. Choose these short-term goals carefully; completing short, fast races as well as longer, endurance-oriented competitions builds speed, stamina and a sense of pace. Be sure to allow yourself enough time to both train and recover – use this chapter to figure out when to schedule these practice races so they don't end up hindering your ultimate goal.

Periodisation

It sounds like a dental procedure, but 'periodisation' simply means breaking your training into distinct blocks of time to focus on developing particular physiologic systems. Many elite athletes divide their training time into four basic phases:

1. Endurance (aerobic)

2. Stamina (aerobic/anaerobic)

3. Speed (anaerobic)

4. Rest/Competition

The idea is to start off training 'long and slow' and gradually work toward 'short and fast', strengthening both aerobic and anaerobic systems along the way. Done correctly, this brings you to the threshold of peak performance just prior to your target race. If there's any secret behind world-class athletic performance, this might very well be it. Time to get to work.

Count the number of weeks between today and the date of the race, then organise that time into four phases: Endurance, Stamina, Speed, and Rest/Competition. Allow two to four weeks for the last phase, and divide the other three phases into equal blocks of time. For example, if the race is in 16 weeks, allow about four weeks each for phases one to three, and four weeks for the rest/competition phase. For a six month cycle, or 26 weeks, allow eight weeks each for the first three phases, two weeks for the last. Add any leftover days to the endurance phase.

Next, plan a workout schedule for each phase according to whether you need to concentrate on speed (for races under 30 minutes) or endurance (for races longer than 30 minutes). Then all that's left is to follow through with the plan and just do it.

Short-distance I.T. v long-distance I.T.
The I.T. peak performance programme has two concentrations:

Short-distance I.T.

Long-distance I.T.

Select either one of these to concentrate on during each phase, depending on the length of your chosen race. Short-distance I.T. is designed to prepare you for competitions under 30 minutes; Long-distance I.T. is geared for events lasting 30 minutes plus. Within these two divisions are various small adjustments that can be made to tailor your workouts even further. For the purposes of specific workouts, we'll assume that your baseline workout time is about 50 minutes (plus another 10 for stretching). If your actual workout time is substantially less or more than this, adjust the following workouts accordingly.

Some abbreviations used in this chapter are as follows:

WU = warm-up (to be done at an easy pace)
CD = cooldown (also done at an easy pace)
I.T. = Interval Training workout
XL = extra long workout
AT = aerobic threshold workout
AR = active rest day
min = minute(s)
sec = second(s)

What if I miss workouts because I'm too busy, ill or injured?

If you have to miss a workout because of a genuine lack of time, try to miss an active rest day. These are mainly designed to be recovery days anyway, so not much will be lost. Missing an occasional 'hard' workout (I.T., AT or XL) is fine too – your fitness level won't plummet if you skip a session here or there. If you need to miss a number of days because you're ill or injured, by all means do so. When you're ready, start back up again gradually with a few active rest days before moving on to the more intense workouts (the first few of these should be scaled back a bit, too). If you're missing workouts because of a lack of motivation, be honest with yourself and reassess your goals, then adjust your schedule accordingly. You don't have to do a workout just because it's on the schedule!

Phase one: endurance training

The physiological goal of this endurance-training phase is to develop more extensive capillary beds and mitochondria so that working muscles are able to use more oxygen (this is known as 'aerobic metabolism'). You build endurance as your body develops natural coping mechanisms in response to the stress, learning to hoard fuel and fluid more effectively, to parcel out energy so that it lasts as long as possible, and to reduce wasted motion so that every stride or stroke is as efficient as possible. Just as important as these physical adaptations are the psychological ones. Putting in the time when your target race is still a good way off helps toughen up mental resolve and hones discipline and willpower, which you will definitely need to succeed. For this reason, Phase one includes two XL workouts and one I.T. workout a week to concentrate on developing aerobic metabolism. Don't be disappointed if you don't improve every single week – nobody does. The human body goes through cycles, so be prepared to have bad patches during which you can't accomplish as much as before. Be patient and you'll eventually see gains.

Here's how phase one looks if you are focusing on short distances:

Phase one: short-distance I.T. programme/XL workouts

The first of your two weekly XL workouts does not actually involve going further at all. Instead, focus on going slightly harder than your baseline aerobic workout, keeping the intensity constant for the whole workout. Finish feeling tired but able to go a bit longer (say, 25 per cent more) if you had to. Over the course of this phase, gradually increase intensity, but be careful not to get too confident and push yourself at race pace yet. At this point, you're just letting your body adjust to moderately faster paces sustained for longer periods of time.

For your second weekly XL workout, gradually increase your workout time to 75 minutes (or 50 per cent longer than your baseline aerobic workout) by the final two weeks of this phase. This extended time/distance may seem like a rather substantial leap within a relatively short period. Just keep the intensity low to moderate and you should be right on track.

Phase one: short-distance I.T. programme/I.T. workouts

Do a single session of interval training each week, with 1-minute repetitions and 2-minute intervals. Use the first few workouts to find the right intensity, then gradually increase the number of repetitions until you're doing about 50 per cent more by the end of the phase. Don't mess with the repetition length or the interval length. Let your body guide each workout and don't push to do more if it isn't ready. Strive to finish each workout tired but able to continue a bit longer if necessary.

Here's a breakdown of the phase one: short-distance I.T. programme.

Day 1:	XL
	WU 5 min
	35 min of continuous faster-paced activity, with increasing intensity over course of phase
	CD 5 min
Day 2:	AR (25–35 minutes at slow pace)
Day 3:	I.T.
	WU 10–15 min
	8 × 1 min reps/2 min rest, increasing to 12 reps by end of phase
	CD 5–10 min
Day 4:	Day off
Day 5:	XL (start at 60 min and build to 75 min at a modest pace by end of phase)
Day 6:	AR
Day 7:	AR
Note:	Active rest days do not change throughout the I.T. competitive edge programme

Here's what to do for phase one if you're focusing on long distances:

Phase one: long-distance I.T. programme/XL workouts

Do two XL workouts a week during this phase. The first workout is the shorter one. In addition to a short warm-up and cooldown, do up to 45 minutes of continuous exercise (for races 30–60 minutes long) or up to one hour (for longer races) at your baseline aerobic workout level of effort. Once you work up to the maximum time, gradually start upping the intensity. Use a workout log to track how you feel from day to day and adjust your workouts accordingly.

The second workout depends on the length of your target race. Let's say it's a 10 km run, which you figure will take more than 30 minutes and less than an hour. With this in mind, you need to gradually increase the duration of your workout until it's 90 minutes long. For events longer than an hour, such as a half marathon or a long bike race, build up to two hours. (Events longer than two hours will be dealt with later in this chapter.) Do these workouts at a modest pace, focusing on just completing the distance.

Note: Don't increase training time by more than 20 per cent in a single week.

Too much additional training time is just asking for burnout or an overuse injury. Aim for the sought-after 'tired but could keep going' feeling, adjusting your time and pace accordingly. If you can't manage to complete a full XL workout at least once during this phase, pick another race so there's extra time to prepare, or spend more time on this phase and shorten phase two and phase three.

Phase one: long-distance I.T. programme/I.T. workout

Do interval training once a week, using one minute reps and two minute intervals. Spend the first few workouts finding the right intensity level, then focus on increasing the number of reps by about 50 per cent over the course of this phase. Stick with the same interval and repetition length – the emphasis here is on getting used to doing a longer workout. Things will get more intense later.

Here's how a long-distance I.T. programme week looks for phase one:

Day 1:	XL
	WU 5 min
	build from 40 to 45 or 60 min, depending on goal, with gradual increase in intensity over phase
	CD 5 min
Day 2:	AR (25–35 min at a slow pace)
Day 3:	I.T.
	WU 10–15 min
	8 × 1 min reps/2 min intervals, increasing number of repetitions to 12 by end of phase
	CD 5–10 min
Day 4:	Day off
Day 5:	XL (build up to 90 min or 2 hours, depending on competition goal moderate effort)
Day 6:	AR
Day 7:	AR
Note:	Active rest days do not change throughout the I.T. competitive edge programme

The last four to seven days of phase one for both short-distance and long-distance I.T. concentrations should be strictly limited to active rest days, so your body can take a breather and absorb the additional stresses being put on it. You'll be itching for action by the end of this recovery week, so try testing yourself with a time trial or a practice race, something a bit shorter or longer than the distance of your target race. If your goal is to run a 10 km, for example, test yourself with either a 5 km, a five mile, or a 15 km race. For psychological reasons, try to avoid competing at your target race distance. At this early point in your training, your performance may fall well short of your expectations, which can be discouraging. Competing at alternate distances also provides some variety you might not otherwise have. Joseph typically runs three or four five km or 10 km races to prepare for an eight mile target race every year in Honolulu. These shorter races are ideal preparation because he can run at faster tempos, yet recover more quickly than he would doing a 15 km or half marathon. No matter what race you ultimately decide to do, take whatever positive things you can from the experience and use them to keep yourself on course towards a future peak performance. Take three or four active rest days or full days off after this race or time trial before starting phase two.

Phase two: stamina training

This stamina-building phase is unique in that it develops both anaerobic and aerobic systems as the body trains to perform at high intensities for extended periods of time. This type of training is similar to the experience of actual competition, geared to teach the body to improve tolerance of lactic acid and fatigue.

Phase two: short-distance I.T. programme/XL workouts

Do one XL workout a week that's 75 minutes long, or 50 per cent longer than your baseline aerobic workout. This maintains a stable aerobic foundation while you work to improve stamina. If you're up to it, you can crank up the intensity a notch, but the most important thing is just to put in the time and complete the entire workout, especially since the I.T. and AT workouts during this phase are often challenging enough.

Phase two: short-distance I.T. programme/AT workouts

An AT (anaerobic threshold) workout is scheduled only once every other week. Some athletes call these sessions 'lactate threshold workouts' because they develop tolerance of lactic acid, that waste product of anaerobic metabolism that makes your legs burn after a hard repetition. The slower it pools in your muscles, the faster you can go for longer distances … and that's what sets PBs and wins races.

An AT workout isn't easy. It's the closest thing to actual racing you'll experience in training. Here's how it works: after a 10 to 15 minute easy warm-up, do 15 minutes at a constant, high intensity, enough so that you're short of breath and unable to speak in full sentences, but not full-out racing. Think of it as a 90 per cent effort and finish feeling like you only have a few more minutes at that intensity left in you. You may have to pause at the end to catch your breath, just as you might do in a race; then do a 10 minute cooldown. Ease up whenever you start feeling overly strained and make a note to start more conservatively next time. As your fitness improves, you'll be able to increase the pace, but never go beyond the point where you feel in complete control of the workout.

Phase two: short-distance I.T. programme/I.T. workouts

There are 2 I.T. sessions a week in phase two. For the first, do the same number of one minute repetitions at the same pace as at the end of Phase one, but now decrease the length of each interval. For example, if your interval was two minutes long, slowly decrease it – to 1:45, 1:30, 1:15 – stopping when you get down to one minute. This may sound like no big deal, but this shorter recovery time makes doing the reps at the same level of intensity a true challenge. If you're really struggling, ease off and take slightly longer intervals. By the end of this phase, you'll want to be doing one minute reps with one minute intervals at the same or a slightly higher level of intensity. Feel tired? Good. You're doing it right.

The second I.T. workout of the week is done on weeks when you don't do an AT workout. Do five high-intensity, three minute long repetitions with three minute intervals (we call these 'three minute drills'). Try to keep the intensity level consistent for all the reps throughout the workout and finish feeling as if you could do one more rep at the same pace if you had to. After finding an intensity level that feels right for you, try to increase it gradually over the course of the phase.

Three minutes of pushing yourself hard is going to seem like an eternity at first. It's long enough to generate a significant amount of lactic acid, but brief enough so that your body can deal with it. These drills will help get you racing fit, ready to handle the challenge of the hard, continuous effort of competition.

Note: Because of the greater level of effort required for this phase, you may need an additional day off occasionally.

Here's how the phase two: short-distance I.T. programme week breaks down:

Day 1:	AT WU 10–15 min 15 min continuous high-intensity effort, intensity increasing over course of phase CD 5–10 min

Alternate week:

Day 1:	3 min drills WU 10–15 min 5 × 3 min reps/3 min intervals, intensity increasing over course of phase CD 5–10 min
Day 2:	AR or day off
Day 3:	I.T. WU 10–15 min 1 min reps with intervals decreasing from 2 min to 1 min over course of phase, same number of reps as end of phase one CD 5–10 min
Day 4:	AR or day off
Day 5:	XL (75 min or 50 per cent longer than baseline aerobic workout, okay to up intensity level)
Day 6:	AR
Day 7:	AR

If you're focusing on longer distances, here's how to do phase two:

Phase two: long-distance I.T. programme/XL workouts

To train for a competition lasting 30 to 60 minutes, do a 90 minute XL workout at a moderate level of effort once a week. For longer races, train with alternating workouts: a 90 minute session one week, a two hour session the next.

Phase two: long-distance I.T. programme/AT workouts

Do this workout every other week. It consists of 20 minutes at a constant, high intensity, enough so that you are short of breath but not full-out racing. Push yourself in a controlled manner and finish feeling like you could keep going another three or four minutes at the same intensity if you had to.

Phase two: long-distance I.T. programme/I.T. workouts

For your first of two weekly I.T. sessions, do the same number of one minute reps at the same intensity as at the end of phase one, but decrease the length of each interval. Slowly reduce it from two minutes to 1:45, then 1:30, then 1:15, stopping when you get down to one minute.

For the second I.T. workout (on weeks when you don't do the AT workout), do five minute drills: five repetitions, each lasting five minutes, with three minute intervals. These longer reps are tough, but they're excellent training for longer races. Slowly increase the repetition intensity over the course of this phase, always finishing feeling as if you could do one or two more repetitions.

Here's how the phase two: long-distance I.T. programme week shapes up:

Day 1:	AT
	WU 10–15 min
	20 min of high-intensity effort, increasing intensity as phase progresses
	CD 5–10 min

Alternate Week:

Day 1:	WU 10–15 min
	5 min drills (5 × 5-min reps/3 min intervals)
	CD 5–10 min
Day 2:	AR or day off
Day 3:	I.T.
	WU 10–15 min
	12–15 1 min reps, gradually decreasing interval from 2 min down to 1 min, same intensity and number of reps as end of phase one
	CD 5–10 min
Day 4:	AR or day off
Day 5:	XL (90 min at moderate pace if preparing for 30–60 min race for longer races, alternate 90 min sessions one week with 2 hour session the next)
Day 6:	AR
Day 7:	AR

Allow four to seven active rest days at the end of this phase. If you're curious to see how you're doing in terms of conditioning, sign up for a practice race or do a time trial on your own at a shorter distance than your target race. Take three or four active rest days or days off after this race or time trial before beginning phase three.

Phase three: speed (anaerobic) phase

This phase takes you from 'racing fit' to 'racing sharp', using larger muscle fibres, improving efficiency and focusing on intensities higher than that of an actual race. The end result: greater ease performing at faster speeds. Better conditioning means less struggle in the early portion of the race, so there's more reserve to kick into another gear as the finish line approaches.

Phase three: short-distance I.T. programme/XL workouts

Every other week, workout 75 minutes or 50 per cent longer than your baseline aerobic workout, whichever is greater (alternate this session with the AT workout).

Phase three: short-distance I.T. programme/AT workouts

Do 15 minutes of continuous high-intensity work at an increasing level of effort over the course of the phase (alternate this session with the XL workout).

Phase three: short-distance I.T. programme/I.T. workouts

Do the first I.T. session of the week with one minute repetitions and one minute intervals. But here's a new twist: to wring more intensity out of this workout, break the reps up into four sets (for example, divide 12 reps into four sets of three repetitions each), rounding off uneven numbers. For each set, do the first two reps at about the same pace as at the end of phase two. Crank it up a notch for the third rep, making sure you stay short of going full tilt. Increase the intensity for all repetitions accordingly over the course of this phase. Keep the same one minute rest period between reps and three easy minutes between sets.

The second I.T. workout of the week will include either:

• Twelve repetitions of 30 seconds, with one minute intervals, or

• Five repetitions lasting two minutes, with three minute intervals.

Aim to do a mix of both workouts during this training period. To prepare for shorter races, emphasise the 30 second reps, or do the longer reps to get ready for longer races. Finish every workout with that 'I could keep going' feeling, tired but not completely exhausted. Again, increase repetition intensity over the course of this phase.

Here's the phase three: short-distance I.T. programme week at a glance:

Day 1:	I.T.
	WU 10–15 min
	3 or 4 × 1 min reps/1 min intervals, with 3 min between sets, final rep in each set done at even greater intensity
	CD 5–10 min
Day 2:	AR
Day 3:	I.T.
	WU 10–15 min
	12 × 30 sec reps/1 min intervals, or 5 × 2 min reps/3 min intervals, depending on target race length
	CD 5–10 min
Day 4:	Day off
Day 5:	XL (75 min or 50 per cent longer than baseline workout, whichever is greater)

Alternate week:

Day 5:	AT
	WU 10–15 min
	15 min of high-intensity effort
	CD 5–10 min
Day 6:	AR or day off
Day 7:	AR

Here's how to do phase three if you're concentrating on longer distances:

Phase three: long-distance I.T. programme/XL workouts
This once a week session should last about 90 minutes, at a moderate pace, if you're training for competitions of 30–60 minutes. For longer races, alternate 90 minute sessions with two hour sessions.

Phase three: endurance I.T. programme/I.T. workouts
Do the first I.T. session of the week with one minute repetitions and one minute intervals. But, to make things even more intense, break the reps up into four sets (for example, divide 12 reps into four sets of three), rounding off uneven numbers. For each set, do the first two reps at about the same pace as at the end of phase two. Increase the effort level for the third rep, staying just short of maximum speed. Do three easy minutes between sets. Remember to increase the intensity over the course of the phase.

For your second I.T. workout of the week, you have a choice of two workouts:

- Five sets of 2 minute reps with 3 minute intervals, or

- Five sets of 5 minute reps with 3 minute intervals.

Find an intensity level that lets you finish feeling tired but able to keep going a bit longer if necessary, then increase that effort level over the course of this phase as your fitness improves.

Here's what the phase three: long-distance I.T. programme week looks like.

Day 1:	I.T.
	WU 10–15 min
	4 sets of 3–4 × 1 min reps with 1 min interval, done at same intensity as at the end of phase two
	CD 5–10 min
Day 2:	AR
Day 3:	I.T.
	WU 10–15 min
	5 × 2 min reps/3 min interval; alternate this with 5 × 5 min reps/3 min intervals, with intensity increasing over phase
	CD 5–10 min
Day 4:	Day off
Day 5:	XL (90 min at moderate pace if preparing for 30–60 min race, or alternate 90 min sessions with 2 hour sessions to prepare for longer races)
Day 6:	AR or day off
Day 7:	AR

You won't need to take any additional active rest days at the end of phase three, since phase four emphasises lighter training in preparation for competition.

Phase four: rest/competition phase

The rest and competition phase tends to be the one that athletes screw up the most. Improved speed, stamina and endurance should have you on the brink of realising your physical potential, but if you're burned out from overtraining, all that hard work is completely useless. Don't sabotage things by training hard right up until race day.

In order to be in peak condition for competition, your body needs adequate rest before race day. Think back to the practice races or time trials you did between phases, how they came after several active rest days, with another three or four easy days or full days off before you advanced to the next phase. During phase four, staying fresh and rested is of even greater importance.

Assuming your target race coincides with the end of phase four, you want to squeeze in one to three time trials or practice races during this phase before the big day arrives. Why test yourself at this stage of the game? Two reasons: it's another opportunity to practise performing at maximum effort, and it provides a chance to achieve personal bests (and a shot of confidence) at a shorter distance than your target race. Unlike in the first two phases, make sure these practice races or time trials are shorter than your target race distance, because longer races require more time for recovery. For instance, if you're planning on a 10 km for your target race, practise with a five km race or a one mile time trial. If possible, try to keep all practice races under 30 minutes, no matter what distance the target race is. If you want to do a longer race, do it between the earlier phases (or, better yet, save it for after you successfully complete your target race).

The mantra for phase four is 'less is more'. For the next three to six weeks, decrease the length of all your workouts by 30 to 40 per cent (even active rest days), while keeping your intensity level the same as in phase three. (Athletes call this 'tapering', and studies show that it is the best way to maintain peak fitness for a window of four to six weeks.) The week of your target race, reduce your workouts by half. You should feel pumped up and fresh at the end of these workouts, not tired. Skip the last I.T. workout and make sure you have at least four days of active rest or days off just prior to the race. This helps keep your body fresh and injury-free.

Here's how a tapering week looks for the phase four: short-distance I.T. programme:

Day 1:	I.T. WU 10–15 min 2 sets of 3–4 1 min reps/1 min intervals, with last rep of each set done at a slightly higher intensity CD 5–10 min
Day 2:	AR (⅔ as long as usual)
Day 3:	I.T. WU 10–15 min 6–8 × 30 sec reps/1 min intervals, or 3 × 2 min reps/ 3 min intervals CD 5–10 min

Note: If target race is on day 7, substitute an active rest day here.

Day 4:	Day off
Day 5:	AR (⅔ as long as usual)
Day 6:	AR (⅓ as long as usual)
Day 7:	XL (45 min at moderate pace) or target race

Here's how a tapering week looks for the phase four: long-distance I.T. programme, with a race on day 7:

Day 1: I.T.
WU 10–15 min
2 sets of 3–4 1 min reps/1 min intervals, with last rep
of each set done at slightly higher intensity
CD 5–10 min
Day 2: AR (⅔ as long as usual)
Day 3: I.T.
WU 10–15 min
3 × 2 min reps/3 min intervals, or 3 × 5 min reps/3 min
intervals
CD 5–10 min

Note: If target race is on day 7, substitute an active rest day here.

Day 4: Day off
Day 5: AR (⅔ as long as usual)
Day 6: AR (⅓ as long as usual)
Day 7: XL (60 min at moderate pace) or target race

What should you do with all the extra pent-up energy you have? Simple – relax and store it up! You're going to need it on race day.

Don't succumb to the temptation to dabble in other physical activities or fill your day with chores or make any drastic changes to your routine right before a big race. Remember, you're not training to train, you're training to race. Take things easy to conserve as much energy as possible and relax for a few days – you'll more than make up for it when it's time to compete. At this point, psychological preparation is just as important as your physical training, so spend your time on the sofa even more productively by doing some mind exercises known as 'visualisation'.

Visualisation: the mental edge revisited

The only way to perform at a maximum level is to have a clear mental picture of what you plan to do before you do it. Elite athletes use this sort of visualisation all the time. Positive visualisation – as well as negative visualisation – provides the mental edge necessary to reach your physical peak.

Positive visualisation is basically a detailed daydream about your upcoming competition that plays over and over inside your head. Say you're getting ready for a big 10 km race. Visualise the race from start to finish: standing on the line, the start gun firing, your legs striding through the early stages, feeling completely in control, pacing yourself well. Picture the midpoint of the race, when you're beginning to feel tired from the effort but able to push hard through the fatigue. Picture moving with strength and confidence, maintaining good form as you move up through the field. Approaching the last stage of the race, the strain is increasing, but you dig in for the final sprint towards the finish. You cross the line, exhausted but exultant.

The secret of successful visualisation is realism. The more details you can include – landmarks, the clothes you're wearing, other athletes, the sound of the crowd – the closer your mental race will be to the real thing. On race day, all you will have to do is physically follow the route your mind has gone over again and again.

Visualise it first, then execute it.

The best way to visualise a race is to view the actual course. Most competitions provide maps in advance, so practise doing the course for one or more of your workouts if you can, or at least drive over it in a car. Where are the hills, the sharp turns, the windy sections, the possible bottlenecks? Set the milometer and pick out some key landmarks, so you know exactly where you are and how far you have to go at every point during the race.

You've probably used elements of positive visualisation in the past without even being aware of what you were doing. Negative visualisation, on the other hand, is less commonly used, even by top athletes. But it's just as worthwhile. A better term for it might be 'plan B visualisation' or 'worst-case scenario visualisation', because you imagine all the things that could go wrong during the race. Anticipating and figuring out how to react and deal with each problem can help avert potential disaster and enable you to perform at your best. What if you start out too fast? Or begin to fade halfway through? Or get bad cramp? Many of these problems are encountered during training, so you'll know from experience to slow down or breathe differently or push on through. Perhaps even more importantly, negative visualisation allows you to accept the fact that you're going to feel bad during the race. Whenever you really exert yourself physically, it's going to hurt, so make a conscious vow before the race not to give up when your body starts screaming to stop. It sounds crazy, but doing this in advance will keep you from squandering time and energy debating the matter in the heat of battle.

Start visualising early, in phase one if you like, and do it at least once or twice a week. It keeps you motivated, especially when you're training hard and the race seems light years away. Practise visualisation before time trials or before between-phase competitions, too, and during phase four, practise it several times a week. All it takes is a few minutes before, during or after a workout or whenever you have some spare time. The one time to avoid doing visualisation is right before you go to sleep. It can get the adrenaline pumping so much that sleep becomes impossible. Remember … you can't do it if you can't imagine yourself doing it!

The 24 hours of race day

Finally, the 24 hours of race day arrives. The tough part is behind you – now it's time to get out there and kick some butt! Get to the start line in fighting form by establishing a set routine for the 24 hours before the race. Find a formula that works for you, then use it before each and every race. This can take some experimenting because what works for your friends won't necessarily be a good fit for you. Use practice races to fine-tune your pre-race routine. Here are a few pointers:

Don't exercise too much the day before a race
Don't make the common mistake of over-exercising the day before the race. Do a brief active rest workout instead – just enough to keep your body loose.

Don't do any strenuous activity the day before a race
Avoid any strenuous activity the day before a race, so you don't risk aching or getting tired. Resting before a race is an excellent way to avoid doing boring, heavy-duty household chores, and we highly recommend it!

Eat a light dinner
You don't want a heavy meal sitting in your stomach at the start line. Skip the steak the night before and eat a light dinner instead. Go for carbohydrates over fat and protein – pasta, soups and salads are all good bets. If you're doing a long event, such as a marathon, eat more carbohydrates for three or four days prior to the race to increase the amount of glycogen stored in your muscles – this can keep you from slumping partway through the race.

Get some sleep
Get a good night's sleep, or try to. But don't worry too much if you end up tossing and turning into the wee small hours – many elite athletes do it too and still manage to compete successfully the next day. Adrenaline should carry you through.

What if I can't handle this training schedule?

Training for competition takes greater dedication – more time, more effort, more discipline, more sacrifices. But if getting an absolute maximum performance out of yourself is your goal, the principles outlined in the I.T. competitive edge programme will get you there. The programme is ambitious, but it's designed so that you control the intensity level at all times, allowing you to finish each workout without completely wiping yourself out. If you're pushed for time or find you just can't handle the load physically, use common sense and scale things back. Do fewer reps for your I.T. workouts and shorten the length of your XL workouts and active rest days. Or redirect your energies toward your I.T. or XL workouts and cut back on the others.

Try to keep the effort level up as high as possible to get the most physiological benefit out of I.T. competitive edge training. A short session is better than no session at all. It won't do as much to improve your conditioning, but it can help you maintain rhythm as your target race approaches.

Wake up early

It's never a bad idea to wake up early. Set your alarm for at least three hours before the race so that your body has time to fully prepare for the effort that lies ahead.

Eat and/or drink something

Experiment well in advance of race day to find out what you can tolerate. Some people want nothing more than clear fluids before a race, such as water or sports drinks. Others like to eat an easy-to-digest snack a couple hours ahead of time, something with around 300 calories. If you have a long-endurance event, it's a good idea to eat a small meal about six hours before the start, just to have some fuel in your system. You might want to stash some dried fruit or energy gel on your bike or in a pocket, too, just in case you run low on sugar during the race. No matter how long or short the race, be sure to drink up – have at least ½ litre of fluid.

Get to the race site early

This allows you enough time to register, if you haven't already done so, and find the toilets. You've trained very hard for this moment, so don't let a late arrival shorten your warm-up. You need every moment.

Warm-up

Do an easy warm-up for five to 15 minutes (more if the race is very short) and a handful of 10 to 30 second sprints at race pace or faster to get the heart and muscles primed for the effort ahead. Why sprint now? Think back to your I.T. workouts and how the first repetition always seems so much more difficult than the next few. Basically, this is because your body would rather kick back and relax than exert itself, so it grumbles a bit as you prod it into action. These pre-race sprints (with walking in between) will get that sluggish first rep out of the way so that you can move at a faster pace from the very beginning. Time your sprints so that you finish about five or 10 minutes before the start of the race.

Plan on having pre-race nerves

It's okay to feel nervous before a race – in fact, it serves an important purpose. Adrenaline is a well-known performance booster and is one reason why competition can help you achieve your physical best. Move about slowly, get to the line, take a few deep breaths, and wait for the gun. You're ready.

Keep a steady race pace

It's easier to maintain a steady race pace when you figure out the 'splits' in advance, knowing exactly how quickly you need to complete each section of the race in order to meet your time goal. This can be tricky away from a measured track or pool, as you need to allow for hills, rolling terrain or inaccurate distance markers (another good reason to check out the course beforehand). But a rough plan is still better than nothing.

Not quite sure of your abilities? Divide the race in half and hold back a bit for the first half, then push more aggressively the rest of the way to the finish.

Congratulate, then evaluate

When the race is over, give yourself a well-deserved pat on the back. Then take a moment to do a postmortem evaluation of your performance, relishing the good parts and learning from those less-than-stellar moments. Were you full of speed at the start but weak at the end? Focus on more XL workouts to build endurance. Was the pace too fast? Concentrate on shorter, faster reps in your I.T. workouts. Problems with hills? Choppy water? Gusty wind? An upset stomach? Make adjustments to your future workouts and pre-race routine to make sure you're prepared for these situations next time.

The I.T. competitive edge programme for multisport competitions

If your ultimate goal is to perform in biathlons (two events) or triathlons (three events), the same I.T. programme training principles still apply. Be sure to realistically assess how much time and energy you can commit to this more ambitious training. Elite athletes devote four to eight hours a day to multisport training; for many of them it's a full-time job! The rest of us make do with squeezing in an hour or two of training time on weekdays, and maybe a bit more on weekends. With this in mind, you might consider alternating activities on weekdays and use the weekends for XL workouts and multisport workouts (intense back-to-back workouts for two or three different sports). A multisport athlete in phase one might train with a 14 day cycle instead of a seven day cycle, just because the workout schedule is so much more complicated. For example, a triathlete's training week might look like the following:

Day 1:	Running: I.T.
	WU 10–15 min
	12 × 1 min reps/2 min jog interval
	CD 5–10 min
Day 2:	Swimming: XL (50 min at increased intensity)
Day 3:	Cycling: I.T.
	WU 10–15 min
	12 × 1 min reps/2 min easy cycling for interval
	CD 5–10 min
Day 4:	AR with slow running
Day 5:	Swimming: I.T.
	WU 10–15 min
	12 × 1 min rep/2 min easy interval
	CD 5–10 min
Day 6:	(weekend) Cycling: 90 min to 2 hours (moderate intensity)
Day 7:	(weekend) Running: 75 min (moderate intensity)
Day 8:	Day off
Day 9:	Cycling: XL (50 min, increased intensity)
Day 10:	Running: XL (50 min, increased intensity)

Day 11:	Swimming: I.T.
	WU 10–15 min
	12 × 1 min rep/2 min easy interval
	CD 5–10 min
Day 12:	AR cycling
Day 13:	Day off
Day 14:	Swimming: XL (75 min, moderate intensity)

Do three intense workouts in a row for each cycle, one for each sport, followed by an active rest day.

These longer cycles work best when they stay flexible – there will be days when you can't use the pool or it's too dark outside to ride safely.

This sample schedule doesn't include any multisport workouts, but these should be done about once every week or two. Multisport workouts shouldn't include two I.T. sessions in the same day or two XL workouts – it's overload for training purposes and can lead to injury. Instead, do an I.T. workout for one sport and a XL workout for the other, and do them in the same order as in an actual competition. It's a tough day of exercise, so be sure the next day is a full day off.

Some athletes like 'double days', doing one workout in the morning and another one later in the afternoon or evening. This is fine on occasion, if you have the time. Just make sure each workout is for a different sport, to prevent overuse injuries, and make one of the workouts no more intense than an active rest session. This will let you build up endurance without grinding your body down completely.

I.T. competitive edge programme for long-distance competition

For distance events lasting more than two hours, such as a marathon or a 100 mile ride, endurance is the thing that will make or break you. Because of this, skip phase three (the speed phase) altogether and divide your training time between phase one and phase two, with three weeks or so set aside for phase four.

Use the phase one: long-distance I.T. schedule to increase your XL workouts to about 75 per cent of your estimated target race time. For example, if you plan to run a marathon in four hours, you need to be able to run for three hours at a modest pace during training. To get there, gradually increase your time each week until you reach two hours; then, increase by no more than five to 15 per cent every other week until you hit the three hour mark. On alternate weeks, continue with two hour sessions.

Here's an 18 week phase one: XL workout training cycle to prepare for a four hour marathon:

Week 1:	1 hour
Week 2:	1 hour 12 min
Week 3:	1 hour 24 min
Week 4:	1 hour 36 min
Week 5:	1 hour 48 min
Week 6:	2 hours
Week 7:	2 hours
Week 8:	2 hours 12 min
Week 9:	2 hours
Week 10:	2 hours 24 min
Week 11:	2 hours
Week 12:	2 hours 36 min
Week 13:	2 hours
Week 14:	2 hours 48 min
Week 15:	2 hours
Week 16:	3 hours
Week 17:	2 hours
Week 18:	3 hours

Note: Never do more than three hours straight training. At around three hours, you reach a point of diminishing returns and you just risk injury. Also, the day after each long session should be a day off to let the body adjust to the increased stress and replenish energy stores.

The other phase one workouts remain the same.

Phase two/XL workouts should alternate weeks between two particular workouts: one session done for the maximum allowed time (such as the three hour session in the above sample); the other done for 90 minutes or half the maximum, whichever is greater. Again, give yourself a full day off after these longer sessions.

The other phase two workouts remain the same.

Remember to skip phase three!

Phase four is the same as the regular long-distance I.T. programme, but you should do only one test race during this phase. Make sure it's short (less than 45 or 50 minutes) and at least two weeks before your target race. The final week prior to your big race should consist of nothing more than active rest days to allow you to accumulate maximum fuel stores for the race ahead.

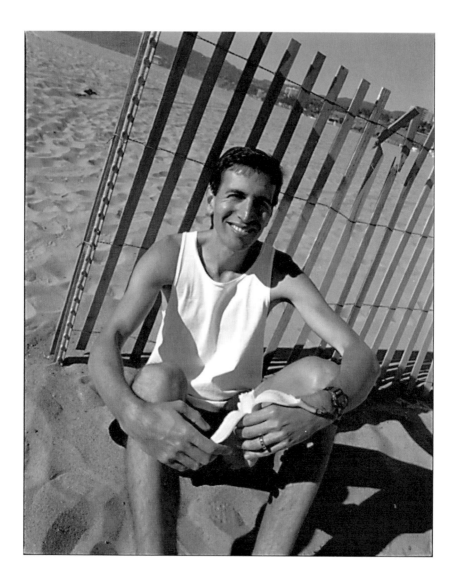

Sample workout log

Keeping track of your workouts can help you to see progress, avoid over-training, and find out what works best for you. Here's a sample page from one of our own workout logs so you can get an idea of how to use one. There are also blank pages for you to photocopy to make your own workout log.

Day/Date: *Monday, 14/8*
Workout: *I.T.*
WU 15 min jog
I.T. 5 x 2.5 min strides/
2.5 min jog
CD 10 min jog
Comments: *feel good !*

Day/Date: *Tuesday, 15/8*
Workout: *AR 20 min run*
Comments: *tired*

Day/Date: *Wednesday, 16/8*
Workout: *I.T.*
WU 20 min jog
I.T. 12 x 30 sec sprints/
1 min jog
CD 10 min
Comments: *still feeling a bit tired*

Day/Date: *Thursday, 17/8*
Workout: *day off*
Comments:

Day/Date: *Friday, 18/8*
Workout: *XL 75 min run*
Comments: *really hot out, but felt strong*

Day/Date: *Saturday, 19/8*
Workout: *AR 20 min easy swim*
Comments: *left ankle sore from running, swim today*

Day/Date: *Sunday, 20/8*
Workout: *AR 20 min run*
Comments: *ankle better today*

(make copies as needed)

Day/Date:_____   Day/Date:_____
Workout: _____   Workout: _____
_____   _____
_____   _____
_____   _____
Comments: _____   Comments: _____

Day/Date:_____   Day/Date:_____
Workout: _____   Workout: _____
_____   _____
_____   _____
_____   _____
Comments: _____   Comments: _____

Day/Date:_____   Day/Date:_____
Workout: _____   Workout: _____
_____   _____
_____   _____
_____   _____
Comments: _____   Comments: _____

Day/Date:_____   Day/Date:_____
Workout: _____   Workout: _____
_____   _____
_____   _____
_____   _____
Comments: _____   Comments: _____

(make copies as needed)

Day/Date:_____   Day/Date:_____
Workout: _____   Workout: _____
_____   _____
_____   _____
_____   _____
Comments: _____   Comments: _____

Day/Date:_____   Day/Date:_____
Workout: _____   Workout: _____
_____   _____
_____   _____
_____   _____
Comments: _____   Comments: _____

Day/Date:_____   Day/Date:_____
Workout: _____   Workout: _____
_____   _____
_____   _____
_____   _____
Comments: _____   Comments: _____

Day/Date:_____   Day/Date:_____
Workout: _____   Workout: _____
_____   _____
_____   _____
_____   _____
Comments: _____   Comments: _____

Glossary

Active Rest Days (AR) Light exercise sessions which allow for recovery between more intense exercise.

Adenosine triphosphate (ATP) A molecule that provides energy for cellular function. It is produced both aerobically and anaerobically and is stored within muscle and other cells.

Aerobic base The initial training phase of the I.T. competitive edge programme, with an emphasis on building mitochondria, capillary density and biomechanical efficiency.

Aerobic exercise Exercise that allows for a continuous supply of oxygen to working muscles; usually done at a moderate intensity that can be sustained for long periods of time.

Aerobic metabolism The primary energy source during long-distance training and racing; the efficient conversion of carbohydrates, fats and proteins, with oxygen, to ATP.

Agonist muscle A muscle that is mainly responsible for contraction within a particular exercise, also known as a 'prime mover'.

Amenorrhea Absence of menstruation.

Anaerobic exercise Intense exercise that overwhelms the available oxygen utilised by working muscles; usually intense physical activity that cannot be sustained for very long.

Anaerobic metabolism The relatively inefficient conversion of carbohydrates to ATP without the assistance of oxygen.

Anaerobic threshold (AT) The level of exercise intensity wherein more lactic acid (a waste byproduct) is produced than can be rapidly 'cleared' by the body. Exercising above this threshold is difficult because lactic acid hinders energy transfer.

Antagonist muscle A muscle that acts in opposition to an agonist muscle.

Baseline aerobic workout The steady, low-to-moderate, comfortably paced exercise performed by most exercisers prior to the I.T. programme.

Calorie Amount of heat required to raise the temperature of one cubic centimetre of water one degree Celsius; the basic unit used to indicate how much potential energy is contained within a given amount of food.

Carbohydrate Nutrient supplying energy to the body, usually categorised as 'simple' (e.g. sugars) and 'complex' (e.g. grains, rice, beans).

Carbo-loading A week long regime that manipulates exercise intensity and carbohydrate consumption in order to store as much glycogen within the body as possible for use during an endurance event, such as a marathon.

Catecholamines Naturally occurring substances such as adrenaline that the body secretes to aid in metabolism and other cell processes.

Cooldown Gradual slowing down of activity after exercise, allowing the body to return safely to a normal state.

Cross training Using a variety of physical activities to build strength, increase motivation and reduce risk of injury.

Dehydration Having less than an optimal amount of water in the body.

Echocardiogram Two-dimensional ultrasound image of the heart, often used by doctors to evaluate heart function.

Efficiency Ratio of energy expenditure to work output.

Electrolytes Minerals found within the body, including sodium and potassium.

Endurance The ability to perform repeated muscular contractions for an extended period of time.

Fartlek A Swedish word meaning 'speed play', similar to interval training except that repetitions and intervals are done in a more flexible, free-form manner.

Fat An essential nutrient providing a source of energy to the body.

Fixed exercise machines Gym-based workout equipment such as stair climbers, stationary bicycles, elliptical trainers, cross-country ski machines and rowing machines.

Flexibility Ability of the joints to move through their full range of motion.

Glucose A simple sugar; the usual form in which carbohydrates are used as a source of energy.

Glycogen Stored carbohydrate in muscle.

Heart rate monitor An electronic device that provides a pulse readout during exercise.

Heart failure Inability of the heart to manage stress.

HGH Naturally occurring anabolic ('building') hormone which stimulates muscle growth by encouraging the creation of protein.

Hydration Taking in fluids to keep the body's water percentage at an optimal level.

Hypoglycaemia Low blood sugar.

Intensity Degree of effort needed to accomplish a particular physical activity.

Interval (or rest) Slower, easier period of recovery between more intense segments of a workout.

I.T. workouts Exercise sessions focusing on interval training, with alternating periods of intense and light activity.

Lactic acid (lactate) A natural waste product of anaerobic energy production, causing temporary muscle fatigue and eventual muscle failure.

Mitochrondria Cell 'powerhouses' containing enzymes needed by the cell to convert food into energy.

Muscular strength The maximum force that can be exerted by a muscle against a resistance.

Myocardial ischemia Lack of oxygen to the heart.

Orthodics Custom-made shoe inserts to support the foot and correct any physical imbalances (e.g. fallen arches).

Overload Applying a greater stress to a muscle or physical system to increase strength or speed; how the body adapts in response to demands applied above a certain threshold.

Overuse injury Injury caused by repeated activity that places too much stress on a particular body part over an extended period of time.

Periodisation A system of varying workout emphasis (endurance, stamina, speed) to attain maximum performance at a desired time.

Plateau effect Levelling off of fitness level after an initial period of gradual improvement.

Progressive overload Applying increased physiologic stress to muscles over a given period of time (days, months, years) to increase strength and fitness.

Protein Essential nutrient made up of amino acids, responsible for building and repairing muscle and other tissues.

Recovery Period of light activity (or no activity) following a race or heavy training, to allow the body to replenish energy stores and repair tissue damage.

Repetition The high-intensity portion of an I. T. workout; a period of greater effort lasting from 30 seconds to about 5 minutes.

Repetition length Duration of a repetition, as determined by either time or distance.

Repetition number Total number of intense segments of exercise completed during an I. T. workout.

R.I.C.E. Basic first aid for many minor exercise-related injuries; an acronym for Rest, Ice, Compression (with an elastic bandage to control swelling), and Elevation (putting injury above heart level to control swelling and pain).

Specificity Training in a particular fashion in order to best perform a similar task.

Stamina Ability to perform at a high intensity for an extended period of time.

Step up/step down method The increased intensity/decreased intensity method of formulating a first I.T. workout.

Strength training Weight or resistance training.

Stress fracture A hairline break in a bone, usually caused by overuse or improper technique.

Stress test Walking or jogging on a treadmill under medical supervision while the heart is monitored for changes.

Stretch reflex Extent to which a muscle can lengthen before it contracts; when a muscle stretches too far, the stretch reflex kicks in and contracts the muscle to avoid further stretching and possible injury.

Subjective assessment (or 'feel') Method of measuring intensity used most often by advanced-level athletes.

Talk test Ability to speak during exercise; a subjective method for measuring exercise intensity.

Time trial An individual race against the clock, performed outside of an organised competition.

Vegan A pure vegetarian who doesn't eat any animal-derived foods, including dairy products.

Warm-up Mild exercise done before stretching or a workout to prepare muscles for more intense exercise.

XL workouts Extra-long exercise sessions, designed to develop endurance and burn calories.

Resources

Recommended reading

Bannister, Roger, and Frederick C. Klein. *The Four-Minute Mile*, New York: The Lyons Press, 1994.

Fixx, James F. *Complete Book of Running*, New York: Random House, 1977.

Parker, John L., Jr. *Once a Runner*, Tallahassee, FL: Cedarwinds Publishing Co., 1998.

Parker, John L., Jr. *Runners and Other Dreamers*, Tallahassee, FL: Cedarwinds Publishing Co., 1998.

Track and Field News

Runner's World

Website sources

Nutrition and Health

www.phys.com
> Helps you to work out your ideal weight, body fat percentage and calorie, fat, protein and carbohydrate needs.

www.nutrio.com
> A US website that provides up to date nutrition news, diet and fitness plans, menus and recipes.

www.webmd.com
> This comprehensive US website has a directory of food topics and advice on many aspects of nutrition and fitness.

www.bbc.co.uk/health
> Healthy living, fitness, nutrition, injury prevention.

www.bupa.co.uk
  Includes information on how swimming, cycling or running can improve your health, as well as other health care advice.

www.bhf.org.uk
  British Heart Foundation.

www.americanheart.org
  Includes self-test for cardiovascular problems and tips on how to avoid heart disease.

www.sportsinjuryclinic.net
  Diagnosis and specialist treatment for injuries.

Cycling:

www.bcf.uk.com
  The website of British Cycling, includes club lists and race results.

www.ctc.org.uk
  Cyclists touring club, includes news, events, shops and local groups.

Running:

www.runnersworld.co.uk
  Magazine, tips, events, injuries.

www.athletics-weekly.co.uk
  Results, profiles.

www.serpentine.org.uk
  Includes advice on all aspects of running including nutrition. Lots of good links.

www.onrunning.com
  News, comments tips, on-line entries.

www.ukathletics.co.uk
  Includes lists of clubs, fixtures & results.

Triathlon:

www.triathletes-uk.org
Lists races, results & clubs.

www.britishtriathlon.org
British Triathlon Association.

www.220magazine.com
Products, events, advice.

Swimming:

www.britishswimming.org.uk
Amateur Swimming Association.

www.swimsearch.com
List of masters swimming clubs throughout the world.

Index